CONTENTS

Introduction

The Water Crisis is the seventy-sixth volume in the **Issues** series. The aim of this series is to offer up-to-date information about important issues in our world.

The Water Crisis looks at concerns about and solutions to the global water crisis.

The information comes from a wide variety of sources and includes:
Government reports and statistics
Newspaper reports and features
Magazine articles and surveys
Web site material
Literature from lobby groups
and charitable organisations.

It is hoped that, as you read about the many aspects of the issues explored in this book, you will critically evaluate the information presented. It is important that you decide whether you are being presented with facts or opinions. Does the writer give a biased or an unbiased report? If an opinion is being expressed, do you agree with the writer?

The Water Crisis offers a useful starting-point for those who need convenient access to information about the many issues involved. However, it is only a starting-point. At the back of the book is a list of organisations which you may want to contact for further information.

*****

Water – the big picture

Information from Eco Schools

Water is a crucial aspect of our lives. We use it not just for drinking and washing but also for industry, agriculture and making almost any kind of product, from hamburgers and tin cans to newspapers and cars.

Our demand for water has grown to the point that the natural water cycle can no longer keep up. Pollution – mainly caused by sewage leaks and chemical discharges – has made clean water a rare and valuable commodity. Climate change may also contribute to making water more scarce.

This means that water organisations have an important role to play in managing, treating and distributing supplies to make sure that our demand for clean, fresh water is satisfied. But this process is expensive – and will become more so as our demand for water grows.

Why water is expensive

Water itself doesn't cost money – but we do pay water companies for recycling water to supplement the natural recycling process of evaporation and rainfall. Water is big business in England and Wales, where water and sewerage services are mainly under private control.

The more we waste water and the more polluted natural supplies get, the harder water companies have to work to make sure we have enough of the clean water we need – which means bigger water bills.

Water companies

Water companies maintain water resources like reservoirs and underground supplies. They are also responsible for treating and cleaning up polluted water, water distribution and supply, sewerage and sewage treatment, river purification, flood prevention and some aspects of coastal protection.

Did you know . . ?

- Less than 2% of the world's water supply is fresh water.
- Taking showers rather than baths would save enough water every week to make 1,000 cups of tea.
- A garden sprinkler uses as much water in half an hour as a family of four in a day.

Most water companies encourage contact with schools. This needs to be handled in an appropriate way. Start by establishing a named contact, then find out what materials and educational or information services they can provide. They may also be able to advise on implementing appropriate aspects of the environmental review.

Water in the world

Saving water is not just about saving money. A sufficient supply of clean water is essential to the health of people and the environment.

In many parts of the world, and even in some parts of the UK, lack of adequate rainfall can make water a scarce resource. In countries where water is difficult to come by and where existing supplies are often contaminated by bacteria or pollution, effective treatment and distribution is literally a matter of life and death.

Rainfall and water distribution

All the fresh water we get arrives as rain. Rough estimates suggest that the UK receives around 250 million cubic metres of rain a year. Similar rough estimates suggest that we use one billion cubic metres a year, i.e. only 0.005% of the total rainfall we receive.

The reason for imposing hosepipe bans in southern England is that some places in the UK get more rain than others. The Thames estuary and much of Essex and Suffolk, the lowlands of the Wash and south to the Cambridge Fens and Bed-

fordshire, and the Vale of York south to Nottingham typically receive less than 60cm of rain a year. At the other extreme, Snowdonia, the Lake District and the western part of the Grampians plus the southern half of the North West Highlands all receive over 320 cm every year.

Most of the rain falls where the population is smallest. The cost of piping enough extra water from areas of high rainfall to the places with high population but low rainfall would be huge. A cheaper method would be to use shorter tunnels to transfer water from rivers carrying water from the wetter west or north into other rivers flowing towards the drier south and east. The effect of adding acidic upland water to mainly alkaline river systems could be to permanently change eco-systems.

The above sum also ignores all the rain for growing crops, keeping our gardens green and our rivers and lakes more or less full of water. If we use too much of the rainfall in any area springs will stop flowing, streams and rivers dry up and lakes disappear. This has happened several times to smaller rivers in the south-east of England in the late 1990s. When a stream, river, or lake dries out all life ceases, from fish to tiny algae. It can be years after the water returns before the full variety of life manages to struggle back.

The water cycle
1. Rain falls, landing on the ground.
2. Rainwater runs off the surface to form streams and rivers or permeates the ground, eventually to form springs.
3. Water travels downstream, finally reaching the sea.
4. Water evaporates from the sea, forming water vapour.
5. Water vapour creates droplets, falling to the ground as rain.

Water consumption and eco-systems
If we take too much water out of rivers, or pump too much up from underground supplies, streams dry up and rivers struggle to support the variety of life they normally hold. A river with a very low flow warms up quicker in the summer – and warm water holds less dissolved oxygen, which makes life harder for creatures to breathe. A low flow of fresh water means there is less water to dilute the treated sewage outfalls that are usually high in dissolved nutrients. This can result in growth of single-celled algae that consume much of the dissolved oxygen in the water as it decays.

Water in manufacturing
Water is required to manufacture a range of products. The following table gives a few examples.

Product	Water required for manufacture
A pint of beer	6 litres
100g jar of instant coffee	8 litres
A newspaper	10 litres
An aluminium can	20 litres
50kg of cement	30 litres
A cotton shirt	150 litres
A car tyre	20,000 litres
The body of a steel car	20,000 litres

■ The above information is from ENCAMS' web site www.eco-schools.org.uk   © ENCAMS

Facts about the global water shortage

- Between 2 to 4 billion people suffer annually from diseases linked to contaminated water.
- An average of 3.5 million people, mostly children under 5, die each year from a water-related disease.
  – Every day over 9,000 people die of water-related illnesses
  – Every hour 400 people die of water-related illnesses
  – Every minute 7 people die of water-related illnesses
- Every 8 seconds someone dies from contaminated water.
- Over the next 20 years, the average supply of water worldwide per person is expected to drop by one-third.
- Some 50 per cent of the population in 'developing countries'– where LIFE is mostly involved – is exposed to unclean, unsafe water sources.
- Asia, Africa and Central America are the three most water scarce regions in the world.
- Water-related diseases have killed more children in the past 10 years than all the people lost to armed conflict since World War II.
- In Africa alone, 85 per cent of all diseases in children under 5 are caused by waterborne illness.
- Water covers 70 per cent of the planet, but only 2.5 per cent of that is fresh water. And less than 1 per cent – .007 per cent – is readily available for human world consumption.
- The average distance the women in Africa and Asia walk to collect water is 6 km or 3.7 miles.
- By 2050, at least one of four people will likely live in countries affected by water shortage.
- One flush of your toilet uses as much water as the average person in the developing world uses for a whole day's washing, cleaning, cooking and drinking.

Cholera facts
- Cholera is transmitted by drinking contaminated water or eating contaminated food.
- Cholera is one of the most dangerous and fatal diseases children and families face in developing countries.
- Cholera can bring death within three to six hours of contact with the bacteria.

■ The above information is from the web site www.missionfeeding.org
© 2003 Life Outreach International

Computer predicts world water shortage

A failure by world governments to address an impending global water shortage will result in food prices rocketing, causing increased disease and malnutrition in developing countries which already spend more than half their income on food.

The grim prediction, made by the International Food Policy Research Institute and the International Water Management Institute, is based on computer modelling which reveals that, by 2025, water scarcity will cause a global drop in food production of 350 million tonnes – more than the entire current US grain crop.

> **'If we continue to take it for granted, much of the earth is going to run short of water or food or both'**

Outlining a doomsday scenario, the report, *Global water outlook in 2025*, adds that a moderate worsening of weather conditions will lead to a 10 per cent loss in the world's grain supply. This would be the equivalent of losing the entire cereal crop of India annually, or the combined annual harvest of sub-Saharan Africa, west Asia and north Africa.

'Water is not like oil. There is no substitute. If we continue to take it for granted, much of the earth is going to run short of water or food or both,' cautioned Dr Mark Rosegrant, lead author of the report and senior research fellow at IFPRI.

At the heart of the problem is the increased competition for water caused by population growth and the spread of urbanisation in developing countries. Water use for households, industry and agriculture will increase by at least 50 per cent over the next 20 years, claims the report, severely limiting the amount of water that is available for irrigation.

The rate at which water is being pumped from aquifers is exceeding the recharge rate, with the situation compounded by the liberal use of fertilisers and pesticides that cause ground water contamination. 'Key aquifers in northern China, northern and western India, west Asia and north Africa will begin to fail' within eight years, claims the report.

Chinese authorities have reported a 6m drop in the water table over the last year in the agriculturally intensive northern plains, where half the country's wheat and a third of its corn are produced.

But it is not just malnutrition that will result from water shortages. Lack of clean water and sanitation are the main causes of disease and child mortality in the developing world. The IFPRI has warned that targets to cut the number of people who lack access to clean water by half, by 2015, set by world leaders at the earth summit in September 2002, are doomed to fail unless governments redirect their water policies.

> **'The world can both consume less water and reap greater benefits but we must act now'**

The report warns that disaster can still be averted but it will require fundamental changes to water policy, such as charging more to affluent people in the developing world to encourage greater water conservation. It also recommends increased investment in crop research and technological improvements to increase food yields from rain-fed farming.

Small-scale irrigation technologies are also part of the solution, with farmers using drip kits or manually operated treadle pumps, allowing them to irrigate crops when water is needed.

'A crisis is not inevitable,' said Dr Rosegrant. 'The world can both consume less water and reap greater benefits but, to achieve sustainable water use, we must act now.'

■ The above information is from Environmental Health News' web site: www.ehn-online.com
© *Environmental Health News* 2003

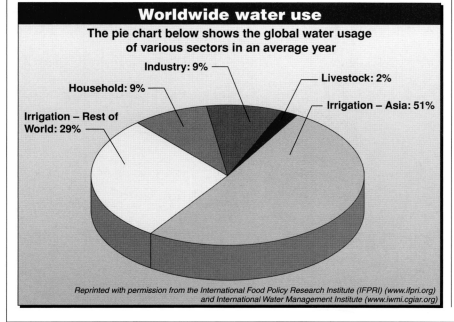

Worldwide water use

The pie chart below shows the global water usage of various sectors in an average year

- Industry: 9%
- Household: 9%
- Irrigation – Rest of World: 29%
- Livestock: 2%
- Irrigation – Asia: 51%

Reprinted with permission from the International Food Policy Research Institute (IFPRI) (www.ifpri.org) and International Water Management Institute (www.iwmi.cgiar.org)

Sustainable world – water

Too much water means flooding, too little and the result is drought and our planet has both in abundance

The figures

According to the latest estimates there are 1386 million km³ (cubic kilometres) of water in the world. 97.7% of this is salt water. Only 2.5% of this is fresh water (about 55 million km³). Of this, 68.7% is permanent ice in the Arctic, Antarctic and Alpine mountains and 29.9% is ground water, mostly deep seated. That leaves 0.26%, or 64,000 km³, of accessible fresh water. On a world-wide scale we withdraw about one-tenth of this water per year. 65% of this water is used in agricultural irrigation.

So, what's the problem?

Between 1960 and 1997, the per capita availability of fresh water worldwide declined by about 60% and another 50% decrease is projected by the year 2025 (Hinrichsen, 1998). The global demand for water is now doubling every 21 years.

Currently there are half a billion people (the collective population of 31 countries) experiencing severe and chronic water shortages. This figure may reach 2.7 billion (nearly one-third of the world's population) in 50 countries by the year 2025. Most of these people will live in Africa and South Asia.

Water tables are now falling in China, India, and the United States, which together produce half the world's food. Water extraction from rivers is reaching crisis point in many places. During the dry season in India, the Ganges River has little water left when it reaches the Bay of Bengal. India is currently pumping up underground water at twice the rate that it is replenished by rainfall. In China, where water tables are falling by 1.5 m per year, the Yellow River runs dry before it reaches the sea for more than half the year. It may or may not surprise Americans that the Colorado River is used so heavily by Colorado, California, Arizona, etc.,
that it is usually no more than a trickle by the time it reaches the Sea of Cortes.

How can this be?

Well, there are three reasons: Firstly that the water isn't in the right places (arid areas account for 40% of the Earth's land masses). Water demands already far exceed supplies in over 80 countries.

Between 1960 and 1997, the per capita availability of fresh water worldwide declined by about 60%

Secondly there is waste. Consider the following: The minimum basic water requirement for human health, including drinking water, is 50 litres per person per day but in the United States the average for domestic usage is 400 litres per person per day – EIGHT times higher.

The minimum amount of water required per capita for food is about

400,000 litres per year. In the USA, the average annual water consumption in food production is 1.7 million litres per capita, 325% more than the minimum requirement.

Thirdly, a lot of the water is unclean. Nearly half the world's major rivers are going dry or are badly polluted. In China, 80 per cent of major rivers are so degraded they no longer support fish life. Much of the pollution is the result of overuse of pesticides in crop production, untreated sewage and toxic chemicals allowed to enter our rivers and lakes. In the developing countries it is estimated that 95% of their untreated urban sewage is discharged directly into surface waters. In the USA the Environmental Protection Agency reported in 1994 that 37% of US lakes were unfit for swimming due to runoff pollutants and septic discharge.

What problems does this cause?

The largest single consumer of water is agriculture (using 65% of all water abstracted from the Earth) and the bottom line is that when water runs out the crops die and people starve.

Also, sanitation in water-deprived areas is poor and preventable water-related diseases in these areas kill an estimated 10,000 to 20,000 children every day. Just give a thought to all that human tragedy.

An important aside

One kilogram of grain requires around 1000 litres of water to grow. It takes 16 kg of grain to produce 1 kg of beef. That's 16,000 litres of water per kg of beef. So, next time you look at a 16-ounce steak on a plate think 'That's over seven cubic metres of water!'

Water

Clean water is readily available in Britain, but worldwide it is becoming scarcer as water tables fall and pollution increases. A massive 1.2 billion people lack access to safe, affordable water and some 2.4 billion lack adequate sanitation.

Water resources

By the year 2025, water shortages could affect two out of three people on the planet.

Between 1990 and 1995, the global consumption of fresh water rose sixfold – a rate more than twice that of population growth. And the current world population of six billion people is expected to swell by three billion in the next 50 years.

Much of this growth will be in the poor countries of sub-Saharan Africa and south-east Asia, already experiencing severe water shortages.

Urbanisation, pollution and climate change are likely to intensify the pressure on water resources and sanitation systems in poorer countries. Also, poor countries lack the resources to combact the effect of water shortages on people, livestock and crops.

The ever increasing demand for irrigation water is a threat to the environment (approximately 40 per cent of the world's food comes from irrigated cropland). Irrigation leads to a fall in water tables and only the wealthy can afford to pump out water from the new depths. Water quality problems are also exacerbated by the build-up of salts in the soil.

Shortages could mean that water-related conflicts become more common as 220 rivers are shared by two or more countries.

Water and health

Half of the world's population are thought to suffer sickness and disease as a result of dirty water or poor sanitation, it is estimated. They are vulnerable to water-borne diseases such as dysentery, diarrhoea, cholera and typhoid.

TEARFUND
CHRISTIAN ACTION WITH THE WORLD'S POOR

To raise standards of healthcare, communities need to understand the benefits of clean water and good hygiene and sanitation practices.

Diarrhoea is preventable, yet in poor countries, some 2.2 million children under five die from diarrhoeal disease every year. Health education as basic as teaching children to regularly wash their hands in clean water reduces rates of diarrhoeal infection by nearly 50 per cent.

Water and women

Every day women and children all over the developing world spend a large amount of their time collecting and carrying water. The weight of water carried can be over 25 kilo-grammes. It is tiring work and the quality of childcare inevitably suffers, as does education if children spend vital school time collecting water.

Water and policy

In 2000, the United Nations agreed a target to halve the number of people without access to safe water by 2015. In 2002 the World Summit on Sustainable Development added a corresponding target on sanitation.

However, the world is not on track to meet these targets due to a shortfall in resources of around £9 billion.

Private Sector Participation (PSP)

Institutions such as the World Bank are promoting PSP as the best way to increase access to water and sanitation.

By the year 2025, water shortages could affect two out of three people on the planet

---

A report published by Tearfund and WaterAid, *New Rules, New Roles: Does PSP benefit the poor?* argues that the private sector is unlikely to be able to provide water to the 1.2 billion people currently lacking it. PSP does not tackle the underlying causes of poor water sources, such as a lack of community involvement.

General Agreements on Trade in Services (GATS)

The governments of poor countries put restrictions and regulations on their services. This is to protect them against foreign companies. The World Trade Organisation (WTO) believes that these regulations restrict trade. The aim of GATS is to remove these restrictions.

GATS would allow multi-national companies access to the markets of developing countries. In developing countries where this is already happening, water is typically more expensive than poor house-holds can afford.

Tearfund and water

Tearfund wants the quality of aid for water and sanitation to be improved. Often money is spent on large infrastructure projects instead of on services that are more beneficial to the poor.

Tearfund is lobbying against PSP. We are also calling on the WTO to discontinue GATS negotiations and keep discussions on essential services, such as water, out of the WTO's agenda.

Tearfund is committed to programmes that involve communities in improving their own sanitation and water supplies. Local people should help to choose a site, the technology used to do the work, and any other aspects of design and construction. They should also be involved in maintaining the site.

■ The above information is from Tearfund. See page 41 for their address details. © *Tearfund*

Water – the facts

Over the past century our water consumption increased tenfold. According to the World Health Organisation, 1.1 billion people have no access to clean drinking water while some 2.4 billion lack proper sanitary provision

Basics

- On our blue planet 97.5% of the water is salt water, unfit for human use.
- The majority of fresh water is beyond our reach, locked into polar snow and ice.
- Less than 1% of fresh water is usable, amounting to only 0.01% of the Earth's total water.[1]
- Even this would be enough to support the world's population three times over, if used with care.[2]
- However, water – like population – isn't distributed evenly. Asia has the greatest annual availability of fresh-water and Australia the lowest. But when population is taken into account the picture looks very different.

Where's it going?

Our increasing thirst is a result of growing population, industrial development and the expansion of irrigated farming. In the past 40 years, the area of irrigated land has doubled.[3]

Signs of stress

- By the mid-1990s, 80 countries home to 40% of world population encountered serious water shortages. Worst affected are Africa and the Middle East.
- By 2025 two-thirds of the world's people will be facing water stress. The global demand for water will have grown by over 40% by then.[1]
- The only ray of hope is that the growth in actual use of water has been slower than predicted.[3]

In sickness and in health

- Dirty water is the cause of numerous diseases, but improving hygiene and sanitation are equally important in order to curb water-related diseases.

Diseases of contamination

There are 4 billion cases of diarrhoea worldwide each year and 2.2 million avoidable deaths – that's a death every 14 seconds.[1] Most diarrhoeal deaths occur in the Majority World and just being able to wash one's hands with soap and water can reduce diarrhoea by 35%.[2]

Insect-related diseases

Malaria, borne by water-breeding mosquitoes, is the biggest killer, causing 1-2 million deaths a year. At any given time 100 million people suffer from the disease.[1]

Parasites

Intestinal worms infect about 10% of the Majority World population. About 200 million people are affected by schistosomiasis (bilharzia), with 200,000 dying each year. After a peak in the late 1980s, guinea-worm infections have been declining as water sources are better monitored.[1, 3]

Needing and getting

The recommended basic water requirement per person per day is 50 litres. But people can get by with about 30 litres: 5 litres for drinking and cooking and another 25 to maintain hygiene. The reality for millions comes nowhere near.

By contrast the average US citizen uses 500 litres per day, while the British average is 200.[2]

The rural poor

People in rural areas are four times more likely than those in cities to have no safe supply of water. The burden falls unequally on women who sometimes have to walk for hours to fetch water. A jerrycan of water with a capacity of 18 litres weighs 20 kilos.

The urban poor

They are less likely than the well-off to be connected to mains water supplies and pay on average 12 times more per litre. In Jakarta, Indonesia, the poor pay water vendors 60 times the price of water from a standard connection; in Karachi, Pakistan, 83 times; and in Port-au-Prince, Haiti, and Nouakchott, Mauritania, 100 times.

Water statistics

Water availability per capita by sub-region in 2000

- Very high
- High
- Medium
- Low
- Very low
- Catastrophically low

Tapping groundwater

Some 97% of liquid fresh water is stored underground in aquifers. People, especially in rural areas, are increasingly dependent on groundwater – up to 2 billion people, a third of the world's population, rely on it.[1]

Aquifers are most severely depleted in parts of India, China, the US, North Africa and the Middle East. It can take centuries for aquifers to recharge, so the world is currently running a groundwater overdraft of 200 billion cubic metres a year.

Pollution is a major problem, resulting from human and farm animal waste, naturally occurring toxins, as well as the over 10 million different synthetic chemicals in use today.

References

1 UNEP, *Global Environment Outlook 3* (Earthscan 2002).
2 Rob Bowden, *Water Supply: Our Impact on the Planet* (Hodder Wayland 2002).
3 Peter Gleick et al, *The World's Water 2002-2003* (Island Press 2002).
4 Worldwatch Institute, *Vital Signs 2001* (WW Norton 2001).
5 Peter Gleick, *The World's Water 2000-2001* (Island Press 2000).
6 Lester R Brown, *State of the World 2001* (Earthscan 2001).

■ The above information is from the *New Internationalist's* web site: www.newint.org

© 2003 New Internationalist

Water statistics

Water use, selected countries, 2000[3]

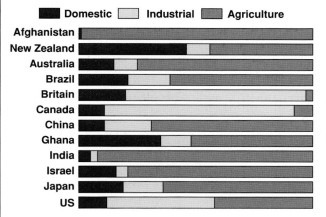

Legend: Domestic · Industrial · Agriculture

Countries listed: Afghanistan, New Zealand, Australia, Brazil, Britain, Canada, China, Ghana, India, Israel, Japan, US

World water use[2]

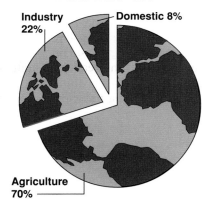

- Industry 22%
- Domestic 8%
- Agriculture 70%

Populations using the least amount of water[3]

Region	Litres of water used per person per day
Gambia	4.5
Mali	8.0
Somalia	8.9
Mozambique	9.3
Uganda	9.3
Cambodia	9.5
Tanzania	10.1

By contrast the average US citizen uses 500 litres per day, while the British average is 200.[2]

Average water (in litres) needed to produce a kilo of food[5]

Potatoes	1,000	Rice	3,450
Maize	1,400	Chicken	4,600
Wheat	1,450	Beef	42,500

Drinking groundwater

Region	% of drinking water from groundwater	People served (millions)
Asia-Pacific	32	1,000 to 1,200
Europe	75	200 to 500
Latin America	29	150
United States	51	135
Australia	15	3
Africa	No data	No data
World		1,500 to 2,000

People without access to a safe water supply, 2000 (in millions)[4]

Region	Rural	Urban	Total
Africa	256	44	300
Asia	595	98	693
Latin America & the Caribbean	49	29	78
Oceania	3	0	3
Europe	23	3	26
North America	0	0	0
World	926	174	1,100

Progress?

Viewed in percentage terms both water supply and sanitation provision have improved in the last decade.

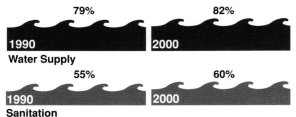

Water Supply: 1990 – 79%, 2000 – 82%

Sanitation: 1990 – 55%, 2000 – 60%

However, the actual number of people in need has barely changed due to the rise in world population.[3]

Global water crisis

Fresh water shortages are a problem that has an impact of some sort on us all. A global problem that demands global solutions

Access to water . . .

As competition for access to water resources increases, the most vulnerable have the least influence.

Governments and companies responsible for the management and allocation of water are prone to conscious or unconscious bias towards the rich and powerful.

The world's poorest people often move to cities in search of employment. As cities grow, the urban poor are most often left with no water supply or sanitation, apart from privately sold exorbitant priced low-quality dirty water.

Dirty water

Millions of people have no choice but to drink water that could kill them. Globally, water-related diseases are the single largest cause of sickness and death, causing a child to die every 15 seconds.

A main reason for this is the lack of adequate sanitation. Despite safe sanitation being just as critical for human health as access to safe water, it gets less attention and funding than water supply.

Water is a resource

Every day each person in the UK uses 150 litres of water, while at the same time, due to water shortages, some of the world's poorest people survive on the equivalent of a 90-second shower!

Population growth is a factor as it is faster where current water shortages are at their worst: in the poorer regions of the world.

Consuming water

It is not just the growing population that is driving the demand for water; consumption is rising due to economic development and growing standards of living.

From 1900-1995 global consumption of water rose six fold; more than twice the rate of population growth.

The rate of consumption is still accelerating; for instance, the expansion of the tourism industry in many developing countries means western-style hotels and complexes swallow up valuable water resources from the local community.

The industrial sector consumes a huge amount of water; for example, every new car manufactured uses 39,090 gallons of water.

Agriculture currently accounts for 70% of global water use.

Growing standards of living add to this pressure. We now eat more beef, pork, poultry, eggs and dairy products, which in turn means a greater demand for grain to feed animals; more grain means more water is needed for irrigation.

An average US diet annually requires 800 kg of grain per person compared to just 200 kg for an Indian diet.

Polluted water

In addition to the effects of poor sanitation water is also polluted by industry and agriculture. The results of this combined pollution cause diseases on a huge scale.

Climate changing water

Climate change is also contributing to the global water crisis, increasing the number of floods and droughts. Again the world's poorest people are the ones most likely to bear the brunt of these natural disasters.

A planned water supply

Globally there is a huge under-investment in this vital resource. This lies at the root of water shortages and inadequate sanitation. Govern-

---

By 2025 it is predicted that two-thirds of the world's population will be living in conditions of serious water shortage

---

ments lack the will, or the capacity, to develop and integrate sustainable water management policies.

A clear solution

Everyone should have the right to water: access to safe and affordable drinking water and adequate sanitation facilities are essential for healthy lives and a sustainable environment.

Some water facts:

- Global consumption of water is doubling every 20 years.
- Available fresh water amounts to less than one-half of 1% of all the water on earth.
- Fresh water is renewable only by rainfall at the rate of only 40,000-50,000 cubic km per year.
- If current trends continue, by 2025 the demand for fresh water is expected to rise by 56% more than is currently available.
- The United Nations reports today that 31 countries face water stress and scarcity. One billion people lack access to clean drinking water.
- Throughout the world, more than one billion people drink unsafe water. 2.4 billion people, 40% of the human race, are without adequate sanitation and 3.4 million people, mostly children, die every year of water-related diseases.
- By 2025 it is predicted that two-thirds of the world's population will be living in conditions of serious water shortage. One-third will be living in conditions of absolute water scarcity.
- The world's quest for fresh water has led to widespread environmental destruction. The number of large dams built to divert water has risen from 5,000 in 1950 to 38,000 today. The environmental

impact resulting from such diversions has been devastating.

- Only 2% of the continental US rivers and streams remain free flowing, they have lost over 50% of that country's wetlands.
- 80% of China's rivers no longer support fish.

The United Nations reports today that 31 countries face water stress and scarcity. One billion people lack access to clean drinking water

- This outline, summarised from *Water Matters*, outlines the main reasons for the growing shortages of the world's most basic resource. The reasons may seem complex but sadly the reality is not; often it is simply a matter of life or death.

Water quality

Background information

Why is water quality important?

Most of the Earth's water is in the oceans (97 per cent) or locked away as ice. The largest volumes of fresh water are stored underground as groundwater, accounting for about 0.6 per cent of the total. Only a tiny fraction (0.01 per cent) is present as fresh surface water in lakes, streams and rivers. But it is this proportion which is so important for many of our terrestrial ecosystems, including humans.

The quality of this fresh water is vitally important. We depend on surface and groundwater sources for our drinking water. We also need water to generate energy, to grow our crops, to harvest fish, to run machinery, to carry wastes, to enhance the landscape and for a great deal more. We use water for washing and cleaning, industrial abstraction, recreation, cooking, gardening and angling, as well as simply to enjoy it. Water is also vital as a habitat for both fresh-water and marine plants and animals.

What causes water pollution?

Many human activities and their by-products have the potential to pollute water. Large and small industrial enterprises, the water industry, the urban infrastructure, agriculture, horticulture, transport, discharges from abandoned mines, and deliberate or accidental pollution incidents all affect water quality. Pollutants from these and many other activities may enter surface or groundwater directly, may move slowly within the groundwater to emerge eventually in surface water, may run off the land, or may be deposited from the atmosphere. Pollution may arise as point sources, such as discharges through pipes, or may be more dispersed and diffuse. Both point source and diffuse water pollution may be exacerbated by adverse weather conditions.

Water pollution

Information from the Geography Site

Everybody needs fresh water. Without water people, animals and plants cannot live. Although a few plants and animals can make do with salt water, all humans need a constant supply of fresh water if they are to stay fit and healthy. Of the total supply of water on the Earth, only about 3 per cent of it is fresh, and most of that is stored as ice and snow at the poles, or is so deep under the surface of the Earth that we cannot get to it. Despite so much of the water being out of reach, we still have a million cubic miles of it that we can use. That's about 4,300,000 cubic kilometers of fresh water to share out between most of the plants, animals and people on the planet.

Whether water is clean enough to use, or too polluted depends on many things such as where it is, whether there is enough for everyone to use, what we do with it, and how we deal with the water we have used before we let it run back to join the rivers and lakes.

The developing world

In the developing world the biggest problem is the shortage of water and the lack of clean supplies. When water is very scarce people have to make good use of it. That might mean using the same source of water for drinking and cooking, a place to wash, a place to clean clothing, pots and pans and a place to let the farm animals drink as well. The same water is used by many people for many different purposes, and each time the water becomes a little more polluted.

Imagine a river that is the only source of water for a series of farming villages along its banks.

The people in the first village might be very careful and always get their drinking water from above the village, do all their washing a little further down stream, and let their animals drink in the river as it leaves their village. By being very careful and aware of basic hygiene they can try to stay healthy. They can do very little to protect themselves from dead animals decaying in the river further upstream, or from germs and parasites introduced to the water by wild animals.

In the developing world the biggest problem is the shortage of water and the lack of clean supplies

---

As the river leaves their village the water will have been polluted by washed bodies, food scraps from washed pots and pans, and body waste from the farm animals and village dwellers. The people in the next village will have to drink this polluted water, and will suffer from the diseases that accompany dirty water.

If an animal dies and falls into the only water supply for miles around, the people still have to drink the water. If the water is thick with mud and snails, but is the only water within reach, people have to drink it.

Whether the water source is a river, a lake or a well, the problems are similar throughout the developing world; little piped and sterilised water, and not enough water to go round means that the same source has to be used for everything, and the risk of pollution and disease is very high.

The developed world

You might think that in developed countries with more money to spend on health care, water supplies and pollution control, water pollution wouldn't be a problem. If people in developed countries lived a life similar to that of people in the developing countries, but used all

their high technology skills, the developed world might have an almost pollution-free water supply. Unfortunately that's not the case. The developed world produces things in factories, people drive around in cars, and want farmers to grow disease- and pest-free crops. The problem is that people in the developed world create far more pollution than their counterparts in the developing world.

Factories can produce huge quantities of pollution that end up in the water supply and it's not just the waste that goes directly into the rivers that causes problems.

The problem is that people in the developed world create far more pollution than their counterparts in the developing world

---

Smoke from chimneys can contain harmful chemicals such as those which create acid rain. When it rains, all these chemicals are brought back down to the ground in the rain drops, and then find their way into the water supply.

Chemicals sprayed onto fields and crops, such as pesticides (to kill insects), herbicides (to kill weeds) and fertilisers (to make crops grow faster, stronger and quicker) can all soak into the soil when it rains. Eventually the chemicals are washed into drainage ditches, streams or rivers, and thus into the drinking water.

Sometimes dangerous chemicals have been dumped in places where they can escape into the water supply. Rubbish dumps and toxic waste sites are all supposed to have a waterproof layer around them to stop chemicals escaping, but sometimes it doesn't work. There are many older dumps where the site isn't waterproof and nobody knows exactly what was dumped there!

Love Canal and the USA

A good example is the Love Canal site near Niagara Falls in the United States of America. During the 1940s

The River Rhine and Europe

The River Rhine is regarded as being Europe's dirtiest river. Almost one-fifth of all the chemical production in the world takes place along its banks. Despite the best attempt to purify the river water before it becomes drinking water, Cornelius van der Veen, the head of the Dutch water works in the Rhine catchment area, once said 'Even well-thought-out purification and reprocessing systems mean that just about every substance present in untreated water is also to be found in drinking water.'

On 1st November 1986, the Sandoz chemical factory in Switzerland had a warehouse fire. While the firemen were extinguishing the flames they sprayed water over drums of chemicals that were exploding due to the heat. The water and chemical mixture was washed into the Rhine, dumping 30 tonnes of pesticides, chemical dyes and fungicides into the river. As a result the river life died up to 100 miles downstream. Things could have been worse though. A nearby building contained sodium, a metal that reacts violently with water. If the fire hoses had been sprayed on the stored sodium, the explosion could have destroyed a group of storage tanks holding the nerve gas, phosgene!

After the fire had been put out, the German government (West Germany at that time) checked the water as it passed through Germany. They discovered a high level of a chemical called Atrazine (a herbicide) that wasn't listed as having been stored at the Sandoz site. Eventually another giant chemical company, Ciba-Geigy, admitted that they'd had an accident the day before and spilled 100 gallons of Atrazine into the river. The West German government didn't believe this figure and stated that nearer to 1500 gallons must have entered the river.

As the monitoring of the Sandoz chemicals continued, more chemicals were discovered and it emerged that many different companies were discharging chemicals unlawfully. BASF, well known for their recording tapes, admitted to spilling 1100kg of herbicide, Hoechst admitted to a major leak of chlorobenzene, and Lonza confessed that they had lost 4,500 litres of chemicals from their plant.

Despite this worrying state over 20 million people were, and still are, getting their drinking water from the Rhine.

---

and 1950s the canal was used as a dump for 22,000 tonnes of chemical waste. The site was then filled in and covered in soil, and houses built over the top. In 1978 it was noticed that many people there were ill and that children were being born with defects. It didn't take long to discover why, and the worst-affected areas were evacuated. Six years later the US government had discovered

another 17,500 similar sites, 546 of which were considered to be dangerous to the health of people living there. At many of these sites, chemicals are leaking out into the groundwater supply causing serious pollution.

Did you know that over 700 different chemicals have been found in US drinking water when it comes out of the tap? The United States Environmental Protection Agency (EPA) classifies 129 of these chemicals as being 'particularly dangerous'.

In 1982 the EPA found poisonous chemicals in the water supply of 35 different states. In 25 states the contamination was so serious that wells had to be closed.

■ The above information is from the web site which can be found at www.geography-site.co.uk

© Geography Site

Water

Universal access to safe drinking water and to sanitary means of excreta disposal were separate decade goals. However, improvements in water supply, sanitation and hygiene can only lead to improved health for children when they go hand in hand

World Summit for Children Goal No. 4: Universal access to safe drinking water

The challenge

Access to adequate water supply is not only a fundamental need and human right. Access to water supply also has considerable health and economic benefits to households and individuals.

On the other hand, the lack of access to adequate water contributes to deaths and illness, especially in children. Thus, the improvement of access to water is a crucial element in the reduction of under-five mortality and morbidity, in particular in poor urban areas.

Access to water also means that the considerable amount of time women and children spend for fetching water could be spent more effectively on other tasks, improving their economic productivity, a key component in poverty-alleviation efforts.

Most frequent diseases related to poor water supply and sanitation:

- Diarrhoea. About 4 billion cases of diarrhoea per year cause 2.2 million deaths, mostly among children under five
- Intestinal worms infect about 10% of the population of the developing world and, depending upon the severity of the infection, lead to malnutrition, anaemia or retarded growth
- Trachoma. About 6 million people are blind from trachoma. Studies found that providing adequate water supply could reduce the infection rate by 25%
- Schistosomiasis. About 200 million people are infected with schistosomiasis, of whom 20 million suffer severe consequences. Studies found that adequate water supply and sanitation could reduce infection rate by 77%

unicef
United Nations Children's Fund

United Kingdom Committee

- Cholera is a world-wide problem, especially in emergency situations, that can be prevented by access to safe drinking water, sanitation and good hygiene behaviours

(Source: *Global Water Supply and Sanitation Assessment. 2000 Report*; UNICEF, WHO, Water Supply and Sanitation Collaborative Council,)

The lack of access to adequate water contributes to deaths and illness, especially in children

Principal transmission routes of disease

Waterbased disease transmission by drinking contaminated water is responsible for significant outbreaks of faecal-oral diseases such as cholera and typhoid and include diarrhoea, viral hepatitis A, cholera, dysentery and dracunculiasis (link to guinea worm).

Water-washed disease occurs when there is a lack of sufficient quantity for washing and personal hygiene, which facilitates, among others, the spread of skin and eye infections e.g. trachoma.)

Diarrhoea is the most important public health problem affected by water and sanitation and can be both waterborne and water-washed. Hygiene promotion which includes the simple act of washing hands with soap and water can prevent one-third of diarrhoeal disease and is therefore key in the prevention of waterborne diseases.

New challenges

During the last decade, new problems that are driven by environmental concerns and socio-economic aspects have emerged. Expanding agriculture and manufacturing business not only increasingly use water but also contribute to pollution of valuable sources of surface and groundwater.

Thus, the overextraction of water has lead to a reduced water table in parts of the world. Problems of contamination of water supplies with naturally occurring inorganic arsenic, in particular in Bangladesh and other parts of South Asia, or fluoride in a number of countries, including China and India, have affected the safety of water supplies.

Water quality

Water purification against bacteria and viruses is still a priority but increasingly threats from hazards not previously known – such as arsenic in groundwater in Asia – require closer monitoring and action.

- For more details on the water environment and its problems and challenges, please visit the UNICEF Water, Environment and Sanitation web site at www.unicef.org/programme/wes/

© UNICEF

store water when rivers flood their banks, reducing downstream damage. Wetland ecosystems are economically valuable to humanity. Robert Costanza, director of the Institute of Ecological Economics at the University of Maryland, estimates the global value of wetlands at close to $5 trillion a year based on their value as flood regulators, waste treatment plants, and wildlife habitats, as well as for fisheries production and recreation.

The world's 6 billion people are already appropriating just over half of all the accessible fresh water contained in rivers, lakes, and underground aquifers. By 2025 humankind's share will be at least 70 per cent – a conservative estimate that reflects the impact of population growth alone. If per capita consumption of water resources continues to rise at its current rate, humankind could be using over 90 per cent of all available fresh water by 2025.

Finding solutions

Caught between growing demand for fresh water on one hand and limited and increasingly polluted supplies on the other, many countries face difficult choices. Finding solutions requires responses at local, national, and international levels. Nothing short of a Blue Revolution in water management can prevent the coming crisis.

Community-led initiatives to manage water resources better can help urban dwellers gain access to safe, piped water supplies, improved sanitation and public health. Despite considerable efforts in the last two decades, the latest assessment by WHO/UNICEF finds that 2.4 billion people are still without an acceptable means of sanitation, while 1.1 billion do not have access to clean piped water.

Up to one-third of all the four billion cases of diarrhoea in the world every year – causing 2.2 million deaths, mostly among children under five – could be avoided if they had access to safe water, adequate sanitation and hygiene, according to *The Global Water Supply and Sanitation Assessment 2000.*

Governments can develop national water-management policies that help not only to improve supply but also manage demand better. Key strategies include regulation of water depending on its end use, watershed management, and appropriate pricing – for example, ending inefficient water subsidies that in effect encourage overuse. There are also huge inequities in the amount spent on improving services to the better-off sections of urban society compared

---

The world's six billion people are already appropriating just over half of all the accessible fresh water

---

to the investments in basic services for the urban poor.

International responses also are important because more than 200 major river systems cross international borders. As long as governments view water problems as national issues, rather than as transboundary issues, conflicts are likely to continue.

International co-operation over sources of fresh water is possible and practicable. In November 1999, for example, Egypt, Ethiopia, and Sudan agreed upon a strategy for 'the sustainable development of the Nile water through the equitable exploitation of the river for the common benefit of all the river basin states'. If fully implemented, the agreement – which covers all uses of the river, for irrigation, hydropower, drainage, drought and flood control, and pollution prevention – would be a significant breakthrough in a water-short region.

Ultimately, national governments in water-short regions will have to come to terms with acute freshwater shortages and accommodate human needs without overusing and polluting available freshwater resources. This will by necessity require a degree of international co-operation not yet seen in the area of resource management.

■ The above information is from *People & the Planet* magazine's web site which can be found at www.peopleandplanet.net
© *People & the Planet 2000-2003*

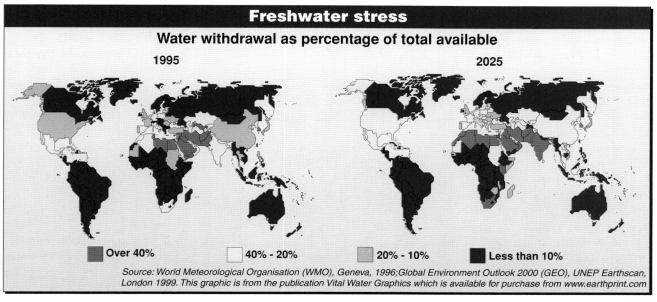

Freshwater stress

Water withdrawal as percentage of total available

1995   2025

Over 40% | 40% - 20% | 20% - 10% | Less than 10%

Source: World Meteorological Organisation (WMO), Geneva, 1996; Global Environment Outlook 2000 (GEO), UNEP Earthscan, London 1999. This graphic is from the publication Vital Water Graphics which is available for purchase from www.earthprint.com

The food and water crisis

Hunger must be reduced without increasing thirst, says WWF

On the eve of World Food Day (October 15, 2003), WWF warned that the farming industry must manage water more efficiently to avoid a water crisis and to meet the world's growing demand for food.

The WWF report highlights that world food production has to be increased to feed an expanding population, with an expected growth of 2 billion people over the next 50 years. Agriculture uses 70 per cent of the world's water, rising to 90 per cent in many developing countries. But only 20-50 per cent of the water withdrawn actually reaches the crops as most of it is lost during transfer to the fields. The report says that many big food-producing countries like the US, China, India, Pakistan, Australia, and Spain have reached or are close to reaching their renewable water resource limits. Water tables are dropping by as much as 10 metres annually in the worst cases, leading to a less reliable supply of water for drinking and sanitation.

'If we do not address the wasteful use of water in farming, this will have serious consequences for achieving the Millennium Development Goal of halving the number of people suffering from hunger by

2015,' said Jamie Pittock, Director of WWF's Living Waters Programme.

The WWF report recommends various methods for managing water more efficiently to tackle the food and water crisis. It highlights that the main causes of water shortages are inappropriate irrigation systems and growing crops unsuited to the environment. This is being driven by misdirected subsidies, low public and political awareness of the crisis, and weak environmental legislation. The WWF report identifies cotton, rice, sugar cane, and wheat as the 'thirstiest' crops in nine large river basins rich in biodiversity.

WWF believes that growing crops more suited to the location and season would give more 'crop per drop'. In the Niger River basin for example, rice is grown in the dry season, and therefore demands more water. Switching to growing wheat during that season could reduce water

use by more than a third on average while still producing a crop of food and commercial value.

The WWF report also suggests that irrigation systems can be improved through better design, regular maintenance, and effective drainage mechanisms. Governments need to allocate water more fairly among farmers where there are shortages. They should also ensure that enough water remains in rivers and wetlands to maintain water supplies, fisheries and wildlife habitats. Altering the natural flow of rivers through dams, for example, may result in decimated fish stocks as the breeding cycles of fish are affected and migration routes are blocked. Freshwater fish are an important source of protein for many of the world's poor.

'Governments must do more than make promises. Together with the food industry and consumers, they must start a new farming revolution – one that ensures there will always be enough food and water for everyone,' said Jamie Pittock.

■ The above information is from WWF-International's web site which can be found at www.panda.org

A matter of life and death

Information from the United Nations

There are more than one billion people who lack access to a steady supply of clean water. There are 2.4 billion people – more than a third of the world's population – who do not have access to proper sanitation. The results are devastating:

- More than 2.2 million people, mostly in developing countries, die each year from diseases associated with poor water and sanitary conditions.
- 6,000 children die every day from diseases that can be prevented by improved water and sanitation.
- Over 250 million people suffer from such diseases every year.

Access to water and sanitation, so crucial for human well-being and development, has now become a priority for the international community. To underscore the need for immediate action, the United Nations has designated 2003 as the International Year of Fresh Water.

Although essential, fresh water is unevenly distributed: while 70 per cent of the world's surface is covered by water, 97.5 per cent of that is salt water. And of the remaining 2.5 per cent that is fresh water, almost three-quarters of that is frozen in ice caps.

While in most regions there is still enough water to meet everyone's needs, it needs to be properly managed and used. In today's world, much water is wasted or used inefficiently, and often demand is growing faster than the supply can be replenished by nature. While competition over water resources can be a source of conflict, history has shown that shared water can also be a catalyst for cooperation.

Key statistics

- About 70 per cent of all available fresh water is used for agriculture. Yet because of inefficient irrigation systems, particularly in developing countries, 60 per cent of this water is lost to evaporation or is returned to rivers and groundwater aquifers.

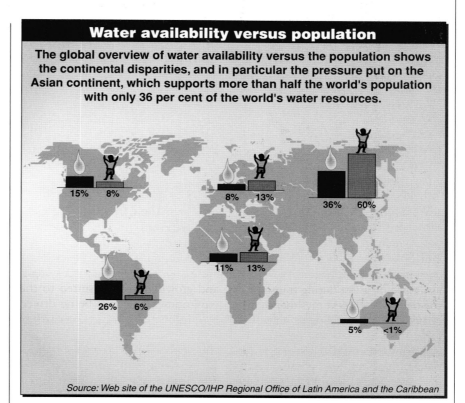

Water availability versus population

The global overview of water availability versus the population shows the continental disparities, and in particular the pressure put on the Asian continent, which supports more than half the world's population with only 36 per cent of the world's water resources.

15% 8%   8% 13%   36% 60%

11% 13%

26% 6%

5% <1%

Source: Web site of the UNESCO/IHP Regional Office of Latin America and the Caribbean

- Water withdrawals for irrigation have increased by over 60 per cent since 1960.
- About 40 per cent of the world's population currently lives in areas with moderate-to-high water stress. By 2025, it is estimated that about two thirds of the world's population – about 5.5 billion people – will live in areas facing such water stress.
- More and more of the world is facing water shortages, particularly in North Africa and Western and South Asia.
- Water use increased sixfold during the last century, more than twice the rate of population growth.

In today's world, much water is wasted or used inefficiently, and often demand is growing faster than the supply can be replenished by nature

- Water losses due to leakage, illegal water hook-ups and waste total about 50 per cent of the amount of water used for drinking in developing countries.
- About 90 per cent of sewage and 70 per cent of industrial wastes in developing countries are discharged without treatment, often polluting the usable water supply.
- Freshwater ecosystems have been severely degraded: about half the world's wetlands have been lost and more than 20 per cent of the world's 10,000 known freshwater species are extinct.
- In areas such as the United States, China and India, groundwater is being consumed faster than it is being replenished, and groundwater tables are steadily falling. Some rivers, such as the Colorado River in the western United States and the Yellow River in China, often run dry before they reach the sea.
- The task of carrying water in many rural areas falls to women and children, who often must

walk miles each day to get water for their family. Women and girls also tend to suffer the most as a result of the lack of sanitation facilities.

- At any one time, half of the world's hospital beds are occupied by patients suffering from water-borne diseases.

- During the 1990s, about 835 million people in developing countries gained access to safe drinking water, and about 784 million gained access to sanitation facilities.

Meeting the global targets

The 147 world leaders who attended the UN Millennium Summit in 2000 adopted the target of 2015 for halving the proportion of people who are unable to reach or to afford safe drinking water. At the 2002 World Summit on Sustainable Development in Johannesburg, countries agreed to a parallel goal to halve by 2015 the proportion of people without proper sanitation.

The cost of upgrading water supply and sanitation to meet basic human needs in developing countries is estimated to run to about $20 billion a year

The cost of upgrading water supply and sanitation to meet basic human needs in developing countries is estimated to run to about $20 billion a year – current spending in those countries totals about $10 billion each year.

Estimates for the level of global investment required in all forms of water-related infrastructure vary widely, although there is wide agreement that the present investment level of $70-80 billion a year needs to be substantially increased. According to some estimates, up to $180 billion is required annually.

While there is agreement on the urgent need to improve water management, there are policy differences regarding how best to do this. Some contend that access to clean drinking water and sanitation is a human right for which governments are obligated to provide services. Others maintain that water is an economic good that should be provided in the most cost-effective way, including market-driven schemes and privatisation of certain components of water delivery as options. Many governments have pursued a hybrid approach.

Countries that have concentrated efforts on improving access to water and sanitation have made progress. In South Africa, for example, 14 million people out of a total population of 42 million lacked access to clean drinking water in 1994. But in seven years, South Africa has halved the number of people who lack access to safe water – ahead of schedule. If the present targets are met, South Africa aims to provide everyone with clean drinking water and sanitation by 2008.

- The above information is from the United Nations Water Year 2003 web site which can be found at www.wateryear.org

© United Nations Department of Public Information

Water facts and figures

- **$2.03bn**: Total western aid earmarked for water

- **$42.5bn**: Total western aid budget

- **£10**: Buys a simple suction pump in Bangladesh to pump water from a reservoir

- **£30**: Pays for the salary of a Bangladeshi hygiene educator for one month, who can deliver hygiene education to 200 slum-dwelling families

- **10%**: The proportion of aid that needs to be devoted to water and sanitation for the UN to meet its targets

- **5%**: The proportion of world aid that actually is devoted to water and sanitation

- **2%**: The proportion of the aid budget of Britain's Department for International Development spent on water projects

- **40bn**: Working hours lost to water-carrying each year in Africa

- **73m**: Working days lost in India due to water problems

- **384,000**: People need to be provided with satisfactory sanitation every day so the UN can reach its targets

- **280,000**: People need to be provided with water every day so the UN can reach its targets

- **52.4%**: The proportion of the Ugandan population with full water access – up from 44.1% in 1997-98 – thanks to concerted government campaign

- **$513m**: The amount Uganda owes its creditors

- **$1.45bn**: The amount that would be needed to provide universal water access in Uganda

- **15 seconds**: The time until the next child dies of a water-related disease

Sourced from OECD, DFID, WHO and UNICEF.
This article first appeared in The Guardian, 2003

Wet world drying

The world water crisis

Summary

The world is facing a water crisis. Freshwater scarcity and pollution are major environmental, economic and political problems facing people in the 21st century. This article considers why water is the new oil, and how the crisis might be averted.

Water, water everywhere – but hardly a drop to drink

Most of the Earth's surface is covered with water in constant circulation through the water cycle. Very little of this water is available to us for drinking purposes. 97% of the Earth's water is salty, contained within seas, oceans and estuaries.

Of the remaining 3%, most is locked away in ice caps or deep underground. Less than one quarter of one per cent of global fresh water is in lakes and rivers. It is from these wetlands that people obtain water.

The world is not short of water in most places . . . but it is becoming very short of usable water.

Nobody's making any more water, and nobody's making any less water. Indeed, there is as much water around today as when dinosaurs roamed the Earth.

It is just that there are far more people around – six billion of us – to drink, poison, pollute, discard and waste water.

One of the problems with water is that it's not evenly distributed around the Earth. Some places have plenty of water, and some have very little. Water supply may be erratic – all the rains may come at once or not at all. Further, water supply and treatment may be badly managed or non-existent.

> *The world is not short of water in most places . . . but it is becoming very short of usable water*

One billion people worldwide have no access to clean drinking water, and 2.9 billion people have no access to water sanitation. Global freshwater consumption rose sixfold between 1900 and 1995 – more than double the rate of population growth. By 2025, two-thirds of humanity may face life in water-stressed conditions.

The United Nations has estimated that one in five countries will experience water shortages within the next 25 years. In South America, only Paraguay has safe water access for over half its population. 22 African countries and 14 Asian ones have safe water access for less than 50% of their populations. Deforestation, irrigation and over-extraction of water in Australia has increased desertification and lowered soil water retention. Many areas of North America and Europe have plenty of water, although the drying of aquifers and wetland drainage is a problem in the Caribbean and south-west USA. Desertification is a problem in parts of Spain, and many European wetlands are heavily polluted.

In the UK, less summer rain, low groundwater, and the shrinking of some aquifers, has led to water

shortages – especially in the Thames Valley, north-west and west England, and Wales.

Freshwater scarcity and pollution are the biggest environmental issues facing the planet. Water is the new oil. We can no longer take water for granted.

Crisis management – possible solutions

There are four main ways of dealing with the water crisis as follows:

Get more
The idea being that if you want more water, get more. This may be achieved by importing water from somewhere with a surplus, or by making water.

Singapore imports its water from Malaysia. California, Israel and Libya all bring water in from outside. This solution only works if neighbouring countries have peaceful relations.

New water cannot be made, but salt can be removed from sea water. There are 7,500 desalination plants worldwide – mostly in the Middle East and dry parts of the USA.

Use less
If you can't get more water, use less. This may be achieved by using water wisely; charging for water use, and/or making existing consumption more efficient.

Using water wisely is the responsibility of everyone from governments to individuals. Dripping taps can be turned off; leaky pipes repaired; showers taken instead of baths; hosepipes used sparingly or not at all.

Pricing mechanisms are used in some countries (like Israel, Australia and the USA) to regulate usage.

Making existing consumption more efficient through the provision of clean water sanitation and wetland conservation, may keep the water crisis at bay.

Have fewer people to use the water
The reasoning here is that fewer people in the world would consume less water. It's a utopian dream but totally unrealistic. Water consumption is growing at twice the rate of human population. Further, the complex and erratic nature of water supply, consumption, population growth and density patterns, do not support this argument.

Fight for it
An extreme option is to steal water from a neighbouring country. Who knows how many of the 21st century's wars will be fought over the ownership of water resources?

■ The above information is from the Wildfowl & Wetlands Trust's web site which can be found at wwwtlearn.org.uk
© *The Wildfowl & Wetlands Trust*

The tide is high

One day, fresh water could be as valuable as oil. Is privatisation the best way to manage the shortage?

The private sector was the first to notice: the planet is running out of fresh water at such a rate that soon it will be the most valuable commodity on earth. Thirty-one countries are facing severe water stress and over one billion people have no access to clean water. Every eight seconds a child dies of water-borne disease. And the crisis is getting worse. By 2025, with an ever-greater number of people sharing the earth's finite supplies of water and its per capita use having more than doubled, two-thirds of the world's people will not have enough water for the basics of life.

On 16 March the third World Water Forum (WWF) will be held in Kyoto, Japan. The WWF is sponsored by the World Water Council, a thinktank whose member-

By Maude Barlow

ship includes the World Bank, global water corporations, the UN, governments and the International Private Water Association. They will decide whether transnational corporations or governments and local communities will control the earth's dwindling supplies.

Thirty-one countries are facing severe water stress and over one billion people have no access to clean water

The second WWF took place in the Hague three years ago. Designed as a showcase for public-private partnerships, it sought to create a 'consensus' among the 5,400 participants that privatisation is the answer to the water crisis. The World Water Council presented a prewritten 'world water vision' endorsing an aggressive for-profit future for water and declared that it is not a basic human right but a need that can be delivered by the private sector.

When the forum closed, a coalition of environmentalists, human rights and anti-poverty activists, small farmers, unions and local communities fighting water privatisation, called the Blue Planet Project, issued a strong condemnation of both the process and the prearranged outcome of the meeting.

Since then, these activists have protested alongside the poor in South Africa, Bolivia and India.

Water for profit takes several forms. Backed by the World Bank and the IMF, a handful of trans-national corporations are seeking to cartelise the world's water delivery and wastewater systems. Already Vivendi and Suez of France deliver private water services to more than 200 million customers in 150 countries. Now they are moving into new markets in the third world, where debt-struck governments are forced to abandon public water services and hand over control of water supplies to for-profit interests.

In Ghana, just the prospect of World Bank-imposed water privatisation resulted in a 95% increase in water fees

These companies have huge profits, charge higher prices for water and cut off customers who cannot pay. There is little transparency in their dealings, they produce reduced water quality and have been accused of bribery and corruption. Based on the policy known as full-cost recovery (charging for the full cost of water, including profits for shareholders) the water companies are able to impose rate hikes that are devastating to millions of poor people who are forced to use cholera-laced water systems instead. In Ghana, just the prospect of World Bank-imposed water privatisation resulted in a 95% increase in water fees.

A new type of water consortium has emerged in Germany that may be a prototype for the future. Companies such as AquaMundo put together giant investment pools using overseas government aid, private bank investments and public utilities funds in the recipient country. In an arrangement called cross-border leasing, they hire local contractors to run the water services. Some investment companies keep their money in tax havens, avoiding national taxes, and offer a deal to cash-strapped governments. In these public-private partnerships, the private investor is guaranteed huge profits from the public purse for many years, and if the company or investment pool disappears, the local government is left holding the bag.

The bottled water industry is growing at an annual rate of 20%. Last year, nearly 100bn litres of bottled water were sold around the world, most of it in non-renewable plastic. Fierce disputes, mostly in the developing world, are being waged between local communities and companies such as Coca-Cola and Nestlé, aggressively seeking new supplies of 'boutique water'. Perrier is being taken to court by citizens in Michigan and Wisconsin in a dispute over licences to take huge amounts of aquifer water that feeds the Great Lakes of North America. In India, whole river systems, such as the River Bhavani in Tamil Nadu state, have been sold to Coca-Cola even as the state is suffering the worst drought in living memory. As one company explains, water is now a 'rationed necessity that may be taken by force'.

Corporations are now involved in the construction of massive pipelines to carry fresh water long distances for commercial sale, while others are constructing supertankers and giant sealed water bags to transport vast amounts across the ocean to paying customers. The World Bank says that 'one way or another, water will soon be moved around the world as oil is now'. All of these forms of water privatisation are protected in international trade regimes like the World Trade Organisation. A recently leaked document showed that the EU has put water services high on its list of demands of other countries in the ongoing General Agreement on Trade in Services talks. This should come as no surprise, as the European water companies are powerful players in the service industry lobby and advise governments and trade negotiators alike in the drafting of these deals.

These are the issues that will dominate the WWF and over which a battle for hearts and minds will be waged. The stakes for a world running out of water have never been higher.

The World Bank says that 'one way or another, water will soon be moved around the world as oil is now'

■ Maude Barlow is a co-founder of the Blue Planet Project and the author, with Tony Clarke, of *Blue Gold, The Fight to Stop Corporate Theft of the World's Water* (Earthscan).

© Guardian Newspapers Limited 2003

Water as a human right

Questions and answers

What are human rights?

Human rights are fundamental rights and freedoms to which every person is entitled, by reason of their humanity. Within the United Nations, States have signed up to the Universal Declaration of Human Rights, which outlines the basic rights to which all people are entitled. States are obliged to respect, protect and fulfil these rights for all citizens, without discrimination.

What is the right to water?

In summary, the right to water, announced on 26 November 2002 by UN Committee on Economic Social and Cultural Rights, puts an obligation on governments to progressively extend access to sufficient, affordable, accessible and safe water supplies and to safe sanitation services to all citizens without discrimination.

Why wasn't there a right to water before now?

At the time when the original Universal Declaration of Human Rights was drawn up, it was assumed that all people would have access to safe water, as it is essential to all life. Consequently water was never named as a human right before now. This has since been shown to be a false assumption, as over a billion people are still without access to safe water. The acceptance of a General Comment on the right to water corrects this assumption.

Is the right to water enforceable?

The acceptance of a General Comment on the right to water outlines the obligations and responsibilities that governments have to ensure that all people have access to safe, sufficient, affordable water. As such it is not a law in itself, but an interpretation of responsibilities. As this right to water is used by governments and citizens, precedents will be set which will pass into law.

The realisation of the right to water will be progressive. States will have an obligation to move towards the full definition of what is safe, affordable and accessible water, but are not expected to achieve this in the first instance

Does the right to water mean water will be free?

The adoption of the General Comment on the right to water does not mean that water must be delivered for free, but must be safe, affordable, accessible and sufficient. This is the same as the realisation of other rights, such as the right to food, the right to shelter and the right to adequate health. However, through the acceptance of a right to water, there is explicit recognition that water is a social, as well as an economic, good.

Does the right to water mean that everyone will now get water?

The right to water is a further tool for citizens and governments to use to ensure that there is universal access to water. This does not mean that overnight all people will gain access to water, but instead means that governments must recognise the indisputable right of all citizens to

---

The right to water demonstrates the recognition of the need and entitlement of all people to access safe, affordable and sufficient water supplies

---

gain access to safe, affordable, sufficient water supplies, without discrimination. Governments will have an obligation to work towards the provision of water. This provides citizens with an entitlement which they can use to lobby governments to deliver water. This does not imply that the other routes which are currently being used to access water should be stopped; the right to water is simply a further tool.

Who else supports a right to water?

The concept of a right to water has been supported implicitly through the UN, with water mentioned as a right within the right to health, the rights of the child and other instruments. Some governments, such as South Africa, have enshrined a right to water within their constitution. Many non-governmental organisations, particularly those which espouse a 'rights-based approach', also support the right to water. Some multi-national companies, such as Suez, also stress that water is a right.

Is sanitation included in the right to water?

Sanitation is included in the right to water – with reference to the rights to health and adequate housing, this document states that, 'States parties [governments] have an obligation to progressively extend safe sanitation services, particularly to rural and deprived urban areas, taking into account the needs of women and children.'

How can/will the right to water be used?

The right to water demonstrates the recognition of the need and entitlement of all people to access safe, affordable and sufficient water supplies. As such, those without access to water will be able to use this right to water to convince decision-makers to prioritise water services.

Will the right to water make a difference to people's lives?

Clearly, the right to water is only powerful if governments and civil society recognise and publicise this new right. If it does not become general knowledge that there is a right to water, people will not be able to use it to assist them to access water services.

How much water is included in the right?

The amount of water that should be available is not specified in the General Comment on the Right to Water. Instead it states that the water must be sufficient, affordable, accessible and safe. These factors vary so much from place to place that there is no fixed amount. If figures were to be specified they could also run the risk of being limiting where the minimum standard is already in place, but an increase in water and sanitation services could further improve standards of health and dignity.

How will a right to water affect WaterAid's work?

WaterAid has been moving towards a rights-based approach to development, which recognises people's needs and entitlements, and their own role in gaining access to these needs and entitlements, such as health and education. This right to water strengthens WaterAid's range of tools for assisting communities to access water, in recognising that water is as important as other entitlements and is also crucial in order to deliver on those other rights and entitlements.

How does a right to water change the lives of poor people?

The existence of the right to water is not going to suddenly change the lives of poor people. However in adopting the right to water, the UN is recognising the importance of water in the improvement of people's living conditions and development. This right now needs to be publicised, and the implications for poor people needs to be fully understood by governments, civil society and any private-sector operator responsible for the delivery of water services.

Over time, the right to water will be used in the same way that other rights have been, such as the right to housing, to protect communities from discrimination, and to ensure a safe, affordable, accessible and sufficient supply of water.

WaterAid has been working with other organisations on interpreting the right to water – what has this involved?

WaterAid has been working with the Centre on Housing Rights and Evictions (COHRE), the World Health Organisation (WHO) and the Centre for Economic and Social Rights (CESR) to produce a publication which will explain what is contained within the right to water, and the implications of this for governments, private companies and civil society. This is due to be published for the International Year of Fresh Water, 2003

How will WaterAid use the right to water?

WaterAid will play an important role in publicising and explaining what is meant by a right to water and how it can be used to benefit poor people and communities. This will be achieved through documents such as the one above, and on a national programme level. WaterAid should be prepared to work with local organisations to inform communities and local governments of the right to water and how it can be used.

Clearly some of WaterAid's partners are going to be more interested in using right to water to assist in delivering essential services than others. Urban non-governmental organisations (NGOs) particularly tend to have a more activist slant to their work than some of WaterAid's more service-delivery orientated partner organisations. However, it is relevant to all organisations, as it sets out some standards and obligations for the delivery of the right to water.

How can benefiting communities use the right to water?

Communities which are working with local partners (NGOs, community-based organisations or private-sector organisations) should be informed of the right to water so that they can use this as an extra tool in their demand for access to a safe, affordable, sufficient water supply. In no way does the right to water replace other approaches which are used by WaterAid's partners through participatory approaches, where communities are given the choice of level of service, and are required to make cost-contributions to the installation, operation and maintenance of water services.

The right to water adds to the tools available for a rights-based approach to development. This emphasises the empowerment of communities, through people-centred development, where communities and individuals have the responsibility to act on their own behalf, and governments are accountable for ensuring that there are no barriers to access to services (such as rules stating that people living in illegal settlements are not able to access services).

■ The above information is from WaterAid's web site which can be found at www.wateraid.org

© WaterAid

The impending water crisis and solutions to avert it

Information from the International Food Policy Research Institute and the International Water Management Institute

If current trends in water policy and investment hold or worsen, we will soon face threats to the global food supply, further environmental damage, and ongoing health risks for the hundreds of millions of people lacking access to clean water. These findings come from *Global Water Outlook to 2025: Averting an Impending Crisis*, a report by the International Food Policy Research Institute (IFPRI) and the International Water Management Institute (IWMI) released on World Food Day.

Using sophisticated computer modelling, the report projects that by 2025, water scarcity will cause annual global losses of 350 million metric tons of food production – slightly more than the entire current US grain crop.

'Unless we change policies and priorities, in twenty years, there won't be enough water for cities, households, the environment, or growing food,' cautioned Dr Mark Rosegrant,

lead author of the report and senior research fellow at IFPRI. 'Water is not like oil. There is no substitute. If we continue to take it for granted, much of the earth is going to run short of water or food – or both.'

Due in part to rapid population growth and urbanisation in developing countries, water use for households, industry, and agriculture will increase by at least 50 per cent in the next 20 years. Increased competition for water will severely limit the availability of water for irrigation, which in turn will seriously constrain the world's production of food.

Declines in food supply could cause prices to skyrocket, and higher prices will lead to significant increases in malnutrition, since many poor people in developing countries already spend more than half their income on food.

'For hundreds of millions of poor farmers in developing countries, a lack of access to water for growing food is the most important constraint

they face,' said Frank Rijsberman, director general of IWMI. 'If countries continue to underinvest in building strong institutions and policies to support water governance and approaches to give better access to water to poor communities, growth rates for crop yields will fall worldwide in the next 25 years, primarily because of water scarcity.'

According to the report, it would take only a moderate worsening in global water policy to bring about a genuine water crisis. If governments continue to cut spending on crop research, technology, and infrastructure, while failing to implement institutional and management reforms, global grain production will drop by 10 per cent over business-as-usual levels, equivalent to losing the entire annual grain crop of India.

Lack of adequate investment and poorly planned systems will hamper progress in providing water and sanitation services for hundreds of millions of people.

'Currently, more than 1 billion people around the world do not have access to a safe water supply, and adequate sanitation is even less available,' noted Dr Joachim von Braun, director general of IFPRI. 'Lack of clean water and sanitation is a major cause of disease and child mortality. While world leaders recently agreed at the World Summit on Sustainable Development to cut in half the number of people without access to clean water by 2015, this goal will not become a reality unless governments redirect their water policies to meet the needs of poor people.'

Fundamental changes in water policies and investment priorities could achieve substantial benefits and sustainable use of water. For example, the report recommends

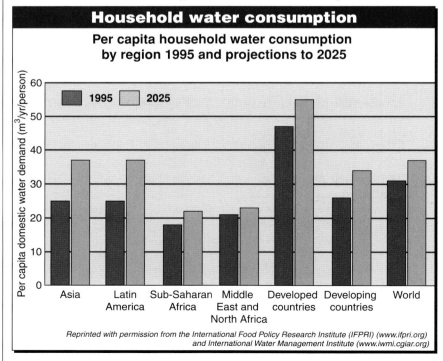

Household water consumption

Per capita household water consumption by region 1995 and projections to 2025

Reprinted with permission from the International Food Policy Research Institute (IFPRI) (www.ifpri.org) and International Water Management Institute (www.iwmi.cgiar.org)

pricing water to reflect its cost and value.

'Although water subsidies are commonplace in developing countries, they tend to benefit relatively wealthy people,' explained Dr Peter Hazell, director of Environment and Production Technology at IFPRI. 'Making affluent people pay for water would encourage them to conserve. It would also free up financial resources to provide clean, safe water to poor people.'

The report also recommends increased investment in crop research, technological change, and rural infrastructure to boost water productivity and growth of crops yields in rainfed farming, which will account for one-half the increase in food production between 1995 and 2025.

'A crisis is not inevitable, the world can both consume less water, and reap greater benefits. To achieve sustainable water use, we must act now'

'We need to invest in water conservation, for example, using innovative low-cost, small-scale irrigation technologies – such as a five-dollar bucket and drip kit or manually operated treadle pumps – that allow smallholder farmers to irrigate crops using less water, and deliver water to crops when it is needed,' said Rijsberman. 'A number of useful new small-scale technologies and community-level water management innovations have emerged in recent years. Governments must learn from these practices in order to implement practical solutions for using less water in agriculture. Without conservation, aquifers, lakes, and wetlands will be further depleted.'

'A crisis is not inevitable,' said Rosegrant. 'The world can both consume less water, and reap greater benefits. To achieve sustainable water use, we must act now. The

required strategies take not only money and political will, but time as well.'

■ The International Food Policy Research Institute (IFPRI) seeks sustainable solutions for ending hunger and poverty.

The International Water Management Institute (IWMI) improves water and land management for food livelihoods and nature.

IFPRI and IWMI are two of the 16 Future Harvest Centres and receive their principal funding from 58 governments, private foundations, and international and regional organisations known as the Consultative Group on International Agricultural Research.

© Reprinted with permission from the International Food Policy Research Institute (www.ifpri.org) and the International Water Management Institute (www.iwmi.cgiar.org)

Saving water

Get involved in your everyday life. A list of ideas on how to make a difference in your everyday life

Kitchen

- When washing dishes by hand, don't let the water run while rinsing. Fill one sink with wash water and the other with rinse water.
- Only run your washing machine and dishwasher when they are full.
- Keep a pitcher of water in the refrigerator or in the freezer to keep it cold. This is better than keeping the tap running until the water gets cold.
- Have your kitchen sink's disposal plumbed to drain into a barrel outside. The nutrient-rich water containing the ground-up vegetable waste is poured onto our vegetable garden and plants in the yard.

Bathroom

- Take short showers! Before you take a shower, install a low-flow shower-head. They aren't expensive and can make a huge difference in your water consumption.
- Turn off the water while you brush your teeth, shave, etc.
- Fill a milk bottle with water and put it in the toilet cistern – this reduces the volume of water used for flushing by 45 litres every day!

Shopping

- Everything relates to water, water makes up many of your fruits and vegetables, be conscious on a daily basis how much water is important in all elements of your life.
- Make environmentally smart choices in your daily life in terms of products. Eat products that come from agriculture that respects the environment and uses little pesticides, chemicals and less water than intensive agriculture.

No matter where you are

- Keep your community clean, recycle and do not litter. You will actually save water!
- Get your friends and families to be water conscious as well! You make the rules in your house!
- In many countries the water is of excellent quality and hence there is no need for drinking bottled water. Drink the water from the tap and save our environment from plastic bottles. If you do buy bottled water, reuse the bottles or buy bigger bottles.

■ The above information is from the International Year of Fresh Water 2003 web site which can be found at www.wateryear2003.org

© 2003 – UNESCO

Prevention of the world water crisis

Cold water poured on idea of business helping thirsty world. By Jonathan Watts

International financiers unveiled a multibillion-pound plan yesterday to prevent the world suffering a water crisis that they warn could be far more catastrophic than the war in Iraq.

The plan, which aims to raise world spending on water from $80bn (£50bn) to $180bn (£115bn) a year, aims to achieve the UN target of halving the number of people in the world without access to drinking water and sanitation by 2015.

Environmentalists and anti-poverty campaigners, however, criticised the plan as a Trojan Horse, designed to allow the private sector to profit from vast construction projects.

The scheme will be formally launched today in Kyoto at the World Water Forum, the biggest environmental conference since the Johannesburg summit last year.

The French president, Jacques Chirac, has said water will also top the agenda at this year's G8 summit in Evian.

Michel Camdessus, the former managing director of the International Monetary Fund, who oversaw the drafting of the report, said: 'The war on the lack of water is more important than the war in Iraq.'

'It will keep going and going, and soon reach dramatic proportions.'

The plan calls for a 'global control tower' to oversee a huge growth in investment in water-related projects. It suggests the construction of more dams, the introduction of loans from international financial institutions to municipal governments, and greater protection for investors and multi-national utility companies from currency risks.

Critics said it focused too much on large-scale funding and not

> **'The war on the lack of water is more important than the war in Iraq. It will keep going and going, and soon reach dramatic proportions'**

enough on small-scale efficiency gains that could reap rewards through community initiatives such as rainwater harvesting.

'The Camdessus report is too much about big bucks,' said Richard Jolly, of the Water Supply and Sanitation Collaborative Council, a UN-mandated organisation which promotes provision of water to the world's poor.

'It fails to emphasise the need for a change in priorities in the water and sanitation sector. We can't just double the amounts [invested], we must restructure,' he said.

Anti-poverty activists said the forum, which is largely sponsored by construction and drug companies, was being used by the private sector.

'These guys have set themselves up as the global high command of water,' said Maude Barlow, the co-founder of the Blue Planet Project, a Canadian campaigning group.

'The Camdessus report is dreadful. It just promotes further public risk and insulates private companies, who admit they are not in the business to help the poor.'

© Guardian Newspapers Limited 2003

Thirst for profits

Are major corporations fit to deliver water to the world? Information from FOE United States/FOE England, Wales & Northern Ireland

An astonishing one billion people worldwide lack access to clean water, while global consumption of water is doubling every 20 years – more than twice the rate of human population growth. In short, the world faces a major water crisis.

Increasingly, multinational water corporations are asserting that they can provide the answer to the world's water needs by delivering new investment to extend services and networks, and to improve quality. Yet in recent years, the rapidly rising level of private investment in water services in both developing and developed countries has been accompanied by an alarming number of incidents involving corporate malfeasance and irresponsibility. Worse, it has often led to rising charges that effectively exclude the poor, even where water and sewerage networks have been ex-tended. Rarely have markets been regulated tightly enough to promote public needs. And the water com-panies have lobbied hard, often through powerful lobby groups, to open up the water market and to have international rules adjusted accordingly.

International financial institu-tions – including the World Bank and IMF – have supported the expansion of these companies' operations globally by pressing countries to privatise their water service systems as a condition for loans and debt restructuring. The World Trade Organisation has also recently begun negotiations to liberalise water services under the General Agreement on Trade in Services (GATS). Meanwhile, investment treaties are being used by water corporations to try to force governments to compensate them for failed water privatisation schemes, and similar investor rights rules are being written into new trade agree-ments such as the Free Trade Area of

Friends of the Earth

the Americas (FTAA). Services and investment negotiations could cement privatisation in those countries that have been forced to privatise their water and also require countries to deregulate their water sectors.

The world of privatised water is overwhelmingly dominated by two French multinationals: Suez (formerly Suez Lyonnaise des Eaux), with US$9 billion of water revenue in 2001, and Vivendi Universal, with $12.2 billion of water revenue in 2001. Both are ranked among the 100 largest corporations in the world by the Global Fortune 500, and between them they own, or have controlling interests in, water companies in over 100 countries and distribute water to more than 100 million people around the world. Other major corporate actors include German water giant RWE and its British subsidiary Thames Water, and US-based Bechtel, which is pro-moting privatisation plans in South America. Another major player, Enron, has recently withdrawn from the scene.

The major water companies are being given increased access to and control over water markets, yet their record has been troubling on many fronts

---

Bribery, high prices and pollution

The major water companies are being given increased access to and control over water markets, yet their record has been troubling on many fronts. Bribery has been endemic to the industry. For most of the past decade, French magistrates have been investigating allegations of corrup-tion against executives of Suez and Vivendi. On three occasions, water executives have been convicted of paying bribes to obtain water contracts in France. The ability of such firms to serve the public interest, rather than being driven to maximise short-term returns to shareholders, is highly questionable

Major controversies have erup-ted over high prices charged by water corporations. Before privatisation, poor households without con-nections often pay high rates for small amounts of water from tankered or carted supplies. But privatisation often dramatically increases the charges faced by those with main water.

In Cochabamba, Bolivia, rates reached as high as 25 per cent of household income for some poor residents. Since 1993, Suez has been the major partner in the privatised utility supplying water to Buenos Aires' 10 million inhabitants, one of the largest water concessions in the world. According to the first independent study of the utility, prices were raised by more than 20 per cent after privatisation. The study reported that many poorer families could no longer afford to pay their water bill. Privatisation contracts also tend to exclude alternative suppliers, such as informal aguateros, who could otherwise offer a competitive service sensitive to local needs as seen in Santa Cruz and in parts of Paraguay.

Major water multinationals have also committed serious environ-mental violations and have failed to provide adequate or sanitary water supplies: Suez, Vivendi, Thames Water (RWE) and Wessex Water (Enron) all were ranked among the top five polluters by the UK Environment Agency in 1999, 2000 and 2001. In Buenos Aires, where Suez operates the major water concession, 95% of the city's sewage is dumped into the Rio del Plata River, causing environmental damage that must in turn be paid for with public funds.

Multinational water companies are being handed increasing control of the world's water. International financial institutions continue to promote these companies' expansion internationally, and international trade agreements will enable the companies to have even greater influence over the water sector. Yet the major water companies have thus far placed private profits before public need, and the international financial and trade institutions have failed to ensure that water privatisation schemes will not harm people and the planet. A significant shift in water policy is needed to protect the poor and the environment.

■ The above information is from *Water justice for all – global and local resistance to the control and commodification of water*, Issue 102 by Friends of the Earth International. See page 41 for their address details.

Priming the public pump

Charities don't have the clout to tackle the world's biggest problem

One in five people in the world don't have access to clean water. Half of us have no sanitation. This leads to constant ill health – millions of children still die from diarrhoea. It means hours of toil for women and girls who are constantly weary, walking miles to fetch water. Girls miss out on school and lack of sanitation leads to humiliation and ill health.

The answer is not more charity or NGO projects. Water and sanitation are not a matter for charity. They are essential for human health and development. If we look back to Birmingham in the 1820s, in the early days of industrialisation, we find child labour, illiteracy, disease and low life expectancy. The big uplift in health and survival came as engineers built systems that provided water and sanitation. This was even more important than improvements in healthcare.

The developing world needs the same. Thousands of water pumps have been provided without the spares or expertise for maintenance. Inevitably they break down and fall into disuse, thus generating cynicism about the usefulness of aid. Hundreds of miles of pipes have been laid without systems to pay people to maintain them and such systems fail and crumble. Well-intentioned projects funded by short-term aid are recipes for constant failure.

In many very poor countries, the slum dwellers pay large sums for

By Clare Short

water delivered by the bucket and the elite receive water at subsidised rates provided by publicly owned companies. And yet, when the World Bank tries to support – say, Ghana – in working out how it might provide and fund water and sanitation services for all of its people, some NGOs raise bitter campaigns about the immorality of reform which they denounce, inaccurately, as privatisation.

Most of those who join these arguments mean well, but there is a deep paternalism in the attitudes they bring. If we examine our own history or that of the countries which have succeeded in bringing development and improved services to their people, they would adjust their outlook. Developing countries need

sustainable systems that can provide and maintain services for their people. Water is needed for human consumption and also for agriculture. Sanitation requires major investment.

We need therefore to concentrate on sharing expertise, using aid to speed up investment in sustainable systems, and encouraging regulatory arrangements that deliver equitable services which make reasonable charges and ensure services are provided to the poor.

There are very rich elites in developing countries. They tend to control the state and bend the public services to their advantage. Defending inefficient and inequitable public services does not help the poor. In fact, water-related diseases are the single largest source of sickness and death in the world and disproportionately affect poor people.

Improved water and sanitation services are crucial to improved health. Research also shows a strong interaction between health and development. The poor are not a constant group of people.

The poor of the world work enormously hard. They constantly improve their lives through their own creativity and hard work. But ill health is a major barrier to the improvement of their lives. Easily preventable and curable illnesses including malaria, TB and diarrhoea cause enormous burdens. A breadwinner who falls ill throws a whole family into poverty. The ill health of children leads to the spending of savings and the sale of animals and tools, thus reducing families to penury. Investment in sustainable systems to provide water and sanitation to all enhances human dignity and economic development.

There has been an important advance in the way support for development is organised. In the past large numbers of donors funded a proliferation of projects – large and small. The consequence of this was often a hollowing out of state capacity, as finance ministries spent their time dealing with aid missions, aid accounts and evaluations and educated staff were poached from government service for better-paid jobs working for aid agencies. Thus useful projects were provided but they tended to collapse when aid funds ceased to flow. The new development framework requires countries to put in place strategies for managing the economy and funding public services

---

Water and sanitation are not a matter for charity. They are essential for human health and development

---

in a way that will measurably reduce poverty. Significant progress has been made in many countries in improving economic growth and the provision of health and education. Few of these strategies have, up until now, made provision for a systematic expansion of water and sanitation services. An effort is needed to explicitly include plans for expanding water and sanitation services in all poverty reduction strategies and identifying funds for investment and training so that services are systematically expanded and are sustainable. This approach does not

meant that it is desirable that all services should be provided by the state. On the contrary, the investment required means that partnerships with the private sector, aid agencies, and NGOs are highly desirable, but the partnerships must be coordinated so the expansion of services can provide for all and give the poor a chance to lift themselves out of poverty.

Current projections are that two-thirds of countries will face severe water strain by 2025. This will lead to considerable suffering and ill health and an increasing risk of conflict over water both within and between states. At the Johannesburg UN summit on sustainable development last September, strong commitments were made to expand provision of water and sanitation services to the poor. Now is the time to deliver on that promise.

■ Clare Short MP is the former international development secretary.
© *Guardian Newspapers Limited 2003*

Supplying water – for a price

Supplying water and sanitation for the world's people is a huge task – and an expensive one. Whether these essential services are best carried out by governments or the private sector is a much-debated question among policy makers, experts and citizen groups. Some background to this debate and key positions are outlined below.

Providing safe drinking water and sanitation to those lacking them requires massive investment – estimated at $14-30 billion per year in addition to current annual spending levels of $30 billion worldwide. As with other infrastructure services such as electricity, telecommunications and transport, most developing countries rely on public sector utilities to finance and operate water and sanitation services. But because of financial and human resource constraints, the results are often low productivity and inefficient

service and coverage. According to the World Bank, technical inefficiencies in power, water, roads and railways alone were estimated to have caused losses of $55 billion a year in the early 1990s – equivalent to one per cent of the GDP of all developing countries, a quarter of their annual infrastructure investment, and twice the annual development finance for infrastructure.

In the late 1980s, urged by international lenders, countries around the world began turning to the private sector, both to take over

the operation of existing infrastructure enterprises and to finance new infrastructure assets. It was argued that private sector financing and management expertise could improve the quality and quantity of infrastructure services. Private financial resources could be tapped and services expanded, while reducing the burden on scarce public resources.

In developing countries, water and sanitation services are often subsidised, traditionally through direct payments to utilities, and are paid for by general taxation. The current investment in water and sanitation in developing countries is about $15 billion annually. According to the World Bank, governments are responsible for close to 75 per cent of financing and the private sector for about 11 per cent, with the remaining 14 per cent of financing coming from external support agencies.

Popular belief generally holds that water is a common good and basic need that can best be provided by the public sector at very low cost. As a result, the full cost of supplying water is seldom charged to consumers. Even where tariffs are charged to industrial users, they are usually based upon average costs and ignore the real costs of externalities such as wastewater disposal, as well as the 'opportunity costs' such as the benefits lost by not pursuing alternative uses of water. One result is that much water is undervalued and wasted, even as the world faces greater and greater water shortages. Without compensation for the costs incurred, developing country governments usually cannot afford to expand their services to all in need, and the poor who are not serviced are often forced to take arduous treks to fetch water and risk becoming sick from unsafe supplies.

Some proponents argue that privatisation of water and sanitation services can address some of these problems. Currently the private sector manages the water system for only 7 per cent of the world population. That figure is expected to more than double by 2015. Private water management is estimated to be a $200 billion-per-year business at present, which World Bank projections show could reach $1 trillion a year by 2021.

Growing criticism

However, the growing involvement of the private sector comes with growing criticisms. Just as when water and sanitation services were managed by the public sector, there are reports of privately-run services wrought with unsafe contaminants, leaky pipes that go unrepaired for weeks, and, notably, price hikes that put poor people in a position of having to choose between food and water. In Cochabamba, the third largest city in Bolivia, prices increased by 35 per cent after a private consortium took over the city's water system in 1999, resulting in protracted street protests. The contract with the private water supplier was rescinded less than a year later.

Even attempts by some developing country governments to adopt private-sector approaches have served as painful lessons. When the South African government tried to end water subsidies in 2000, the result was that millions of poor people were forced to use water from polluted rivers and lakes, causing one of the country's biggest cholera outbreaks ever.

These cases reinforce two common perceptions – that private-sector participation enriches a few at the expense of many, and that water flows to those who can pay. Critics say that private companies, in their attempt to make attractive bids for long-term contracts, often underestimate the cost of maintaining a water system. Once the contract has been won and operations begun, they resort to cutting staff and maintenance costs, raising prices, or both, to turn a profit. Other detractors of privatisation argue that water is a human right and everyone should be ensured equal and adequate access on a non-profit basis. It should not be managed by for-profit enterprises.

Finding solutions

However, no matter who manages this key resource, water supply and sanitation will inevitably have to be paid for by someone, whether consumers or taxpayers. Some experts argue that private enterprises, which in many cases are in a better position to identify gaps and provide needed services, have an important role to play. But working with the private sector does not mean that a government would, could or should simply hand over the management of its water resources to the private sector, and let the profit motive run its course. Rather, it implies a dialogue among government, the private sector and all users, to come up with equitable and environmentally sound solutions.

A spectrum of relationships could evolve, with many different options for the role of the private sector. Governments could transform their role from the exclusive financiers and providers of infrastructure services to facilitators and regulators of services provided by private firms. Contracts would have to be well designed, with the right balance of minimum standards and penalties, as well as incentives. In all cases, the government must be engaged in both oversight and overall regulation.

Better pricing of water by governments is another proposal considered to be a potential solution. Developing pricing schemes that meet social, technical, economic and environmental concerns is a major challenge. One option being tested in some countries is for governments to pay part of the water bill for poor households that meet certain criteria under a direct subsidy approach. Beyond the basic minimum, consumers would have to pay increasing tariffs per unit used. This would be an alternative to allowing the price of water to fall below economic costs indiscriminately.

■ The above information is from the United Nations Department of Public Information.

© United Nations

Water bills to rise 70%

Bosses demand hike as the network ages

Water bills in parts of the country could soar by 70 per cent over the next five years, it was revealed yesterday.

A report from water regulator Ofwat showed that bills are set to rocket if privatised companies are given free rein.

The average amount would rise by just over 30 per cent between 2005 and 2010, taking the figure from £234 to £306.

But millions of families in the North West and other areas face even steeper increases in bills which have risen sharply since privatisation in 1990.

Customers of United Utilities would see demands go up from £234 to £416, an increase of £173 or 71.2 per cent. Further big increases of at least 35 per cent are threatened for the customers of Southern Water, Anglian Water and Northumbrian Water.

The firms insist huge price rises are needed to repair ageing sewers and mains, and to improve the quality of drinking and river water.

However, consumer groups last night condemned the proposed rises, saying they would hit poorer families and pensioners particularly hard.

Watervoice, the official customer body, said planned works range from welcome investment to prevent sewer flooding and improve the reliability of pipes and sewers, to compliance with little-understood European legislation such as the Shellfish Waters Directive.

Chairman Maurice Terry said: 'The bill for environmental improvements should be shared between everyone who benefits, and not funded exclusively, as now, by water customers.

'Under current arrangements, too many water customers will be paying too much for improvements which have too little benefit for them.

'For example, how many pensioners do we see surfing in wetsuits

By Sean Poulter, Consumer Affairs Correspondent

off the Cornish coast? Yet pensioners in the South West are facing a 22 per cent rise in average water bills.'

He added: 'The bill for Network Rail and the main line upgrades do not fall exclusively on the customer base since they are regarded as a "national priority" and are funded appropriately.

A report from water regulator Ofwat showed that bills are set to rocket if privatised companies are given free rein

'The most recent figures were £3.6 billion for rail ticket sales compared to Government subsidy of £3.8 billion. Why is water different?'

Ofwat warned of hefty rises in water bills if improvement programmes, likely to cost £20 billion, are confirmed. Its director general, Philip Fletcher, who will have a key role in deciding prices, said: 'Hard choices will have to be made about the size of the programmes the firms are expected to carry out if we are to set price limits recognised by customers as appropriate and necessary.

'Ministers will have some difficult decisions on whether all of the proposed drinking water quality and environmental improvements are essential.

'If the programmes of works which each company will be expected to deliver remain unchanged from those set out in the draft business plans then there can be little doubt water bills will need to rise substantially.'

Pamela Taylor, chief executive of Water UK which represents the firms, defended the increases.

She said: 'The industry has achieved significant success, reflected in dramatic improvements in rivers, bathing water, drinking water quality and in our capacity to disappoint cynics expecting hosepipe bans in the heatwave at the start of the month.

'To secure this success we need to continue to invest. We can't let things slip.'

Ofwat will announce what it believes the price rises should be in July next year.

© *The Daily Mail*
October 2003

What they may charge

	2004/05	2009/10	Increase
United/North West	£243	£416	71.2%
Northumbrian	£202	£279	38.1%
Anglian	£277	£379	36.8%
Southern	£251	£339	35%
Welsh	£275	£350	27.2%
Thames	£196	£240	22.4%
South West	£334	£407	21.8%
Severn Trent	£210	£248	18.1%
Yorkshire	£237	£278	17.3%
Wessex	£264	£296	12.12%
England/Wales	£234	£306	30.7%

Source: Ofwat

Water bill could benefit wildlife sites

Information from English Nature

Over 10% of England's Sites of Special Scientific Interest (SSSIs) rely on good and clean supplies of water and so stand to benefit from the proposed changes in the draft Water Bill published in February 2003. English Nature estimates that over 350 nationally and internationally important wildlife sites are affected by water abstraction. English Nature welcomes the proposed Bill as it will provide greater protection of the environment from the impacts of water abstraction.

Man is a heavy user of the limited water resources we have in England. Changes in the world's climate are affecting the seasonal supply of water, making its management more and more critical.

English Nature believes that by having a comprehensive overview of the demands for water, we can plan more effectively to move away from the 'boom and bust' scenario created by winter flooding followed by summer droughts across the country. The proposed changes to regulating abstraction will improve the balance between supply and demand and help to secure adequate protection for wildlife sites.

Hans Schutten, English Nature's freshwater adviser, said, 'Our wildlife depends on a delicate balance of water throughout the seasons and the effects of too little water at the wrong time of year can be devastating to fish such as salmon and trout who rely on good flow of water in our rivers, or birds such as bittern that need a good supply of food in the reed beds they inhabit.

'By licensing all significant abstractions as proposed in the Water Bill, it will ensure that there is a level playing field where all abstractors have to abide by environmental regulations.

'It should also help to solve the problems where current over-abstraction damages wildlife sites.'

Other measures English Nature would like to see in the Bill include:

- By 2012 all abstraction licences, new and existing, should be time limited with resources made available to help conversion;

> *Changes in the world's climate are affecting the seasonal supply of water, making its management more and more critical*

- A clear condition in the renewal of any licences that a check be made on environmental impact;
- The provision of more power to the Environment Agency to enforce its abstracting regulations and endorse sustainable water management;
- An explicit duty for all water companies to conserve water and to manage water sustainably;
- An explicit duty for the new 'Water Services Regulation Authority' and the associated consumer council to further the conservation and enhancement of SSSIs (as already applies to other public bodies under the CROW Act (2000).

You can find the bill published at www.publications.parliament.uk/pa/pabills.htm

■ English Nature champions the nature conservation of wildlife and geology in England. We are advisers to Government on nature conservation and wildlife protection. We work with a range of organisations and individuals in partnership to enhance biodiversity and create opportunities for people to enjoy and experience our natural heritage.

■ The above information is from English Nature's web site which can be found at www.english-nature.org.uk

A global water crisis

Information from WWF International

What is the problem?

The world is facing a freshwater crisis. People already use over half the world's accessible fresh water, and may use nearly three-quarters by 2025. Over 1.5 billion people lack ready access to drinking water and, if current consumption patterns continue, at least 3.5 billion people – nearly half the world's projected population – will live in water-stressed river basins in just 20 years.

On top of this, contamination denies some 3.3 billion people access to clean water, and 2.5 billion people have no water sanitation services. In developing countries an estimated 90 per cent of wastewater is discharged without treatment into rivers and streams. Each year there are about 250 million cases of water-related diseases, with some 5-10 million deaths.

> *Freshwater eco-systems, which harbour the world's greatest concentration of species, are amongst the most vulnerable on Earth*

It is not only people who are threatened by water shortages and pollution. Freshwater ecosystems, which harbour the world's greatest concentration of species, are amongst the most vulnerable on Earth. Half the world's wetlands have been destroyed in the last 100 years. Two-fifths of the world's fish are freshwater species – and of these, 20 per cent are threatened, endangered, or have become extinct in recent decades. The WWF *Living Planet Report* for 2002 shows that the continuing decline of animal species is greater in fresh water than in any other habitat, signalling that one of the underlying causes of the freshwater crisis is the continuing degradation of land and water ecosystems.

WWF's Living Planet Index indicates a loss of over half the world's freshwater biodiversity since 1970. Despite this, the freshwater ecosystems continue to disappear or be altered at an alarming rate. Threats to these ecosystems include conversion of wetlands to other uses – many countries are under pressure to develop floodplains and other wetlands for agriculture or industry; large infrastructure projects such as dams and canals which threaten to alter riverflows; misuse and over-exploitation of water resources, sucking rivers dry and often resulting in depletion of aquifers and falling water tables; introduction of non-native species, which can choke waterways and become health hazards by providing breeding grounds for mosquitoes. Asia's rivers average 20 times more lead than rivers in the industrialised world, and average 50 times more bacteria from human faeces than the World Health Organisation guidelines allow.

The lack of basic environmental resources can exacerbate racial and ethnic tensions, raising the prospect of water wars. Major water sources, such as the Euphrates in the Middle East and the Limpopo in southern Africa, have the potential to ignite conflict if those nations upstream choose to divert water for their own resources at the expense of those living downstream.

Freshwater use is not just an issue in developing nations. Spain, for example, is pushing for a Hydrological Plan that will involve the creation of many dams and reservoirs that would threaten as many as 86 Special Protection Areas and 82 Sites of Community Interest, as designated under the European Wild Birds and Habitats Directives. The Yellow River in China, Colorado River in North America, and the Murray River in Australia are amongst the Earth's major rivers that are regularly sucked dry.

> *Two-fifths of the world's fish are freshwater species – and of these, 20 per cent are threatened, endangered, or have become extinct in recent decades*

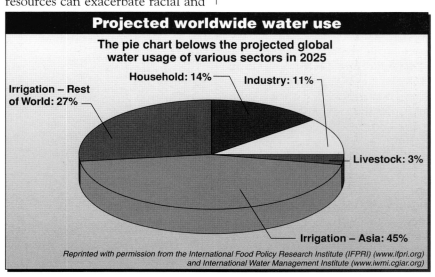

Projected worldwide water use

The pie chart belows the projected global water usage of various sectors in 2025

Household: 14%
Industry: 11%
Irrigation – Rest of World: 27%
Livestock: 3%
Irrigation – Asia: 45%

Reprinted with permission from the International Food Policy Research Institute (IFPRI) (www.ifpri.org) and International Water Management Institute (www.iwmi.cgiar.org)

Water is an issue that affects us all. Humans are already appropriating more than half of all accessible surface-water runoff and this may increase to 70 per cent by 2025. The three largest water users in global terms are agriculture (70 per cent), industry (20 per cent) and municipal or domestic use (10 per cent). At the same time, degradation of water sources is an ongoing problem. It leads to less fresh water being available, and is largely due to poor management of river basins. Culprits include deforestation and over-grazing, which leads to more erratic water runoff and desertification.

Water diversion and inefficient water use are also an issue. Irrigated agricultural systems that consume 70 per cent of the world's diverted water, lose up to 80 per cent of this water through leakage in earthen channels and inefficient application onto fields. In developing countries up to half the water delivered to cities is lost in leaking pipes.

How can this problem be addressed?

WWF is convinced that a successful World Water Forum needs to address three key challenges, calling for an ecosystem approach to water management. Stakeholders must take action to:

- Invest in ecosystem health. The Forum should call upon national governments, multilateral organisations, and the global donor community to recognise that water scarcity, disaster mitigation, and risk management are not always best addressed by infrastructure development.
- Provide food security and alleviate poverty. The Forum should call for sustainable management

of freshwater fisheries to be incorporated as a key component of all water resource management programmes. A commitment to use water more efficiently, especially in agriculture, is essential to make limited water supplies stretch further to meet the needs of people and nature.

- Implement integrated river basin management (IRBM) to support water services. Without a commitment to implementing IRBM, there is danger that progress in providing access to water services will be curtailed by over-exploitation and degrada-tion of the freshwater ecosystems that are the ultimate source of the water. This should include establishing river basin management organisations for more than 261 basins shared by more than one country. Operationalising the World Commission on Dam's guidelines for new dams projects is a key requirement for good river management.

■ The above information is from WWF-International's web site which can be found at www.panda.org

Frequently asked questions about water

Shouldn't the water companies be doing more to save water?
Yes, they should. As a result of growing pressure from the public and government, many water companies are beginning to take this responsibility more seriously. For example, companies are having to spend much more money on fixing leaks in their supply pipes.

But it is also up to everyone to do their bit – on average each of us uses the equivalent of 6,500 buckets (55,000 litres) every year!

My garden is my pride and joy. Will I have to skimp on watering it?
It is possible to keep your garden looking good while using less tap water. For example, watering your plants at sunset, rather than in the heat of the day, means that the water has the chance to get to the roots rather than simply evaporating.

Surely the odd water shortage doesn't hurt?
Unfortunately it does, particularly when combined with drier weather. As we demand more water, the water companies are having to extract more from existing underground reservoirs which are not being refilled by rainfall, and from rivers which are already running low.

This has two main effects. Many species of wildlife, such as otters and butterflies, suffer as too much water is drained away, affecting their natural habitat. And low river levels increase the concentration of pollutants in the water. This also means that there is less oxygen for the plant and animal life.

Does having a water meter help?
Water meters can save money, as you only pay for the water you actually use. They also help you to keep tabs on your water use and on whether you have any leaks. If your house is large with just a few people, or if you don't have a garden, you may find a water meter works for you. Some water companies will install them for free, or give you a trial period so that you can find out whether it will save you money.

■ The above information is from Global Action Plan's web site which can be found at www.globalactionplan.org.uk or www.ergo-living.com

Sustainable water

Information from Sustainable World

How can I help conserve water?

- Don't leave taps running unnecessarily.
- In summer store drinking water in the refrigerator. Don't let the tap run while you are waiting for cool water to flow.
- Wash fruit and vegetables in a bowl rather than under a running tap and use the leftover water to water house plants.
- When cooking don't use more water than you need in saucepans. It not only wastes water but energy too.
- Don't leave the tap running while you brush your teeth or shave.
- Bathing uses 20% of household water consumption. Take showers rather than baths. A five-minute shower uses one-third of the water you'll use for a bath.
- Reduce the amount of water you use to flush your toilet. If you don't have a special low-flush cistern then you can reduce the volume you use per flush by placing a brick wrapped in a plastic bag into the bottom of the cistern.
- Dripping taps can waste up to 5 litres of water a day. Replace any worn tap washers.
- When using your washing machine always try to make up a full load, as the half-load programmes use more than half the water and energy of a full-load programme.
- When using a dishwasher wait until you have a full load before starting the cycle. Incidentally, a new dishwasher uses only 40% of the water of hand-washing a comparable amount (older models use about 60%).
- Wash your car with a bucket and sponge. This uses much less water than using a hosepipe.

In the garden

- Collect the water from your bath/shower (known as 'grey water') to use on your garden.
- Use water butts to collect the rain water from your roof for watering your garden.
- Water your garden in the early morning or evening. This gives the water a chance to get down into the soil before the Sun's heat starts to evaporate it away from the surface. Besides, it's detrimental to your plants' health to cover the leaves with water drops in a strong sun.
- Fit your hose with a trigger device so that you can direct water only to areas of the garden that need it.
- Don't cut your lawn too short in the summer. Longer grass gives shade to the soil surface and reduces the water loss by evaporation.
- Try planting up garden beds with flowers and shrubs that thrive in hot and dry conditions such as rosemary, thyme, evening primrose, rock rose, red hot pokers, Californian poppy, African and Peruvian lilies, pinks, lavenders, buddleia and hebes.
- Mulch beds with material like wood chips, bark, compost or gravel to help prevent water evaporation (and also suppress weed growth).
- When planting trees and shrubs include a vertical section of pipe (guttering downpipe is perfect for this) in the hole so that water can be directed down to the roots rather than the surface. Oh, and make sure you put a good layer of mulch over the refilled hole (but not into the water pipe).

- The above information is from Sustainable World's web site: www.sustainableworld.org.uk

© Sustainable World

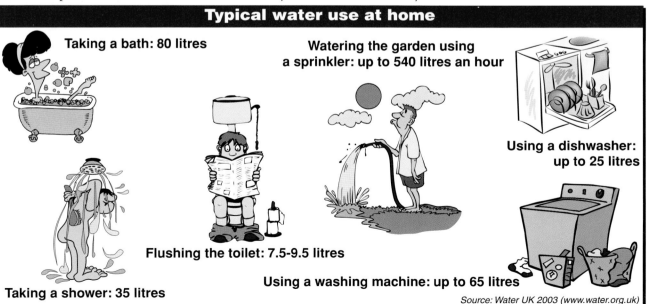

Typical water use at home

Taking a bath: 80 litres

Watering the garden using a sprinkler: up to 540 litres an hour

Using a dishwasher: up to 25 litres

Flushing the toilet: 7.5-9.5 litres

Taking a shower: 35 litres

Using a washing machine: up to 65 litres

Source: Water UK 2003 (www.water.org.uk)

Waterwise in the home and garden

Information from the Environment Agency

The present long spells of hot sunny weather may be doing wonders for your tan, your mood and perhaps even your golf handicap, but it also has an effect on our water supplies.

Even in a country with a cool climate such as the UK, water is a limited resource. During hotter periods, shortages can quickly develop if we do not use water sparingly, particularly in more vulnerable parts of the country, such as the South East. So, are you using your water wisely?

Each year England and Wales receives on average enough rainfall to cover its entire area to a depth of 900 mm. But two-thirds of this water either evaporates or is used by trees, crops and other growing plants. We can't use all of the remaining water because we need to leave enough in our rivers and streams to protect aquatic plants and animals.

Climate change experts predict that we will experience more extreme weather patterns, with wetter winters and drier summers. As a result, there will be less and less clean water available when we need it most.

By following our top tips for saving water in the home and garden, you will soon be on the way to being 'waterwise'. And if you have a water meter, you'll be saving money as well as the environment.

Top tips for saving water in the home

By thinking carefully about your water use in the home and changing some water-wasting habits, it is easy to save water.

- Vegetables and fruit should be washed in a bowl rather than under a running tap and the leftover water can be used for watering house plants.
- Use the minimum amount of water required when you boil water in saucepans and kettles; that way, you'll save energy as well as water.
- Try keeping a bottle or jug of water in the fridge instead of running taps until the water runs cold.
- Half-load programmes on dishwashers and washing machines use more than half the water and energy of a full load. Therefore, wait until you have a full load before switching the machine on.
- Try not to leave the tap running while you brush your teeth, shave or wash your hands, as this can waste up to 5 litres of water per minute.
- A 5-minute shower uses about a third of the water of a bath. But remember that power showers can use more water than a bath in less than 5 minutes.
- Old toilet cisterns can use as much as 9 litres of clean water every flush. Reduce this by placing a 'save-a-flush' or 'hippo' in the cistern.
- Cotton wool and tissues should be put in a waste bin rather than flushed down the toilet.
- Dripping taps can waste up to 4 litres of water a day. Replace worn tap washers for a quick and cheap way of saving water.
- Burst water pipes can cause serious damage as well as waste water. Ensure your water pipes and external taps are lagged in time for the cold winter months.

Top tips for saving water in the garden

In England and Wales it is possible to have a beautiful garden without using any mains water. The following top tips will help you to stop wasting water in the garden:

- Watering in the cool of the early morning or evening helps to reduce evaporation losses.
- If plants and shrubs are watered too often they will remain shallow rooted, weakening the plant. Leave them alone until they show signs of wilting.
- You can use a watering can to water plants with rainwater collected in water-butts. If you prefer to use a hosepipe, fit a trigger nozzle to control the flow.
- Careful weeding and hoeing ensures that watering helps plants and not weeds.
- Plant flowers and shrubs that thrive in hot and dry conditions such as thyme, evening primrose, rock rose, Californian poppy, pinks, lavender, buddleia and hebes.
- Mulches such as wood chips, bark and gravel help to prevent water evaporation and also suppress weed growth, saving you both water and time spent weeding.
- Lawns can survive long periods of dry weather if the grass is not cut too short. Even if the grass turns brown, it will quickly recover after a few days of rain.
- Decking, gravel, paving and cobbles can make an attractive alternative to water-thirsty lawns and have the extra benefit of being low maintenance.
- Garden sprinklers can use as much water in an hour as a family of four uses in a day. If you use a sprinkler, many water companies require you to have a water meter fitted.
- Washing your car with a bucket and sponge uses much less water than using a hosepipe.
- If you prefer to use a car wash, find one that recycles the water.

■ The above information is from the Environment Agency. See page 41 for their address detail.

Water conservation in schools

Information from the Environment Agency

How much money can my school save?

Chesswood Middle School in Worthing fitted a range of water-saving equipment, including urinal controls and self-closing push taps. As a result, not only did the school's water consumption drop by 73 per cent, but they also saved £3,000 on their annual water bill.

Financial savings depend on many issues such as size of school and age of buildings. Some water-efficiency measures cost money to implement, but many cost little or nothing at all.

How do I go about saving water?

Reducing your school's water consumption is a straightforward process and there are many organisations that can help and advise you.

The Environment Agency has a range of free publications on water efficiency, from how to carry out a simple water audit to information on the different water-efficient technologies available.

The DFES suggests that typical annual water consumption in schools is 4 cubic metres (m^3) per pupil per year and this can easily be reduced to 2.85 cubic metres (m^3) per pupil per year.

Watermark is a government-funded initiative that can provide help and advice on benchmarking and water management.

Your water supply company will also be able to provide you with information on how best to reduce your school's water consumption.

Financial savings depend on many issues such as size of school and age of buildings

How can I get my pupils involved?

By focusing on water as a precious and vital resource, children can investigate and think about the ways in which they use water both at home and at school.

There are numerous links between water and the National Curriculum, including Geography Key Stages 2 and 3, Science Key Stages 2 and 3, Citizenship Key Stage 4, as well as Art & Design, Welsh, English and History.

Water in the school is a web-based resource that aims to reduce school expenditure, conserve water and enhance the requirements of the National Curriculum in Mathematics, IT, Citizenship and Key Skills. Visit their web site at www.waterintheschool.co.uk

■ The above information is from the Environment Agency's web site which can be found at www.environment-agency.gov.uk Alternatively, see their address details on page 41.

© The Environment Agency 2003

Every drop counts

Information from CREATE

Last summer CREATE carried out a survey on water conservation in schools, on behalf of the Environmental Agency. Energy and water management professionals were also invited to complete the survey. This was to help ensure that anyone and everyone who is involved in supporting the efficient use of water in UK schools had their say!

Three main outcomes of the study are:

School personnel lack awareness of the potential for savings in water consumption and costs

Water meters in schools are often inaccessible, making the careful monitoring of water consumption a difficult task

Schools lack finance to install water-saving measures.

In response to these outcomes the Environment Agency is working with the DEFRA, DfES, Ofwat, Water UK and The Buying Agency (managers of the *Watermark programme), to identify ways to help schools manage their water more efficiently. CREATE has also been involved in the discussions and will keep you informed of progress through Energy Watch. Remember – fix dripping taps and identifying leaks, they can be very costly!

Visit www.environment-agency.gov.uk for more advice on how to save water and for curriculum resources for schools and colleges.

*Watermark is a government-backed programme to develop a computerised water monitoring database system that will provide the public sector, including schools, with benchmarks and targets for lowering water consumption.

For further information go to www.watermark.gov.uk

■ The above information is from CREATE's web site which can be found at www.create.org.uk

© 2003 CREATE – Centre for Research, Education and Training in Energy

KEY FACTS

- Our demand for water has grown to the point that the natural water cycle can no longer keep up. (p. 1)

- Less than 2% of the world's water supply is fresh water. (p. 1)

- One flush of your toilet uses as much water as the average person in the developing world uses for a whole day's washing, cleaning, cooking and drinking. (p. 2)

- 'The world can both consume less water and reap greater benefits but, to achieve sustainable water use, we must act now.' (p. 3)

- Between 1960 and 1997, the per capita availability of fresh water worldwide declined by about 60% and another 50% decrease is projected by the year 2025. (p. 4)

- Between 1990 and 1995, the global consumption of fresh water rose six fold – a rate more than twice that of population growth. (p. 5)

- It is estimated that half of the world's population are thought to suffer sickness and disease as a result of dirty water or poor sanitation. (p. 5)

- Climate change is also contributing to the global water crisis, increasing the number of floods and droughts. (p. 8)

- The world's quest for fresh water has led to widespread environmental destruction. The number of large dams built to divert water has risen from 5,000 in 1950 to 38,000 today. (p. 9)

- Access to adequate water supply is not only a fundamental need and human right. Access to water supply also has considerable health and economic benefits to households and individuals. (p. 12)

- Water- and sanitation-related diseases claim the lives of over two million children a year. (p. 13)

- Children are the most vulnerable to diseases which result from dirty water and poor sanitation. (p. 13)

- Available freshwater supplies are not distributed evenly around the globe, throughout the seasons, or from year to year. (p. 15)

- Up to third of all the four billion cases of diarrhoea in the world every year – causing 2.2 million deaths, mostly among children under five – could be avoided if they had access to safe water, adequate sanitation and hygiene. (p. 17)

- More than 2.2 million people, mostly in developing countries, die each year from diseases associated with poor water and sanitary conditions. (p. 19)

- About 70 per cent of all available fresh water is used for agriculture. Yet because of inefficient irrigation systems, particularly in developing countries, 60 per cent of this water is lost to evaporation or is returned to rivers and groundwater aquifers. (p. 19)

- Most of the Earth's surface is covered with water in constant circulation through the water cycle. Very little of this water is available to us for drinking purposes. 97% of the Earth's water is salty, contained within seas, oceans and estuaries. (p. 21)

- There are four main ways of dealing with the water crisis as follows: get more, use less, have fewer people to use the water and fight for it. (p. 22)

- In Ghana, just the prospect of World Bank-imposed water privatisation resulted in a 95% increase in water fees. (p. 23)

- The World Bank says that 'one way or another, water will soon be moved around the world as oil is now'. (p. 23)

- Fundamental changes in water policies and investment priorities could achieve substantial benefits and sustainable use of water. (p. 26)

- 'A crisis is not inevitable, the world can both consume less water, and reap greater benefits. To achieve sustainable water use, we must act now.' (p. 27)

- Water and sanitation are not a matter for charity. They are essential for human health and development. (p. 30)

- Current projections are that two-thirds of countries will face severe water strain by 2025. (p. 31)

- Providing safe drinking water and sanitation to those lacking them requires massive investment – estimated at $14-30 billion per year in addition to current annual spending levels of $30 billion worldwide. (p. 31)

- Man is a heavy user of the limited water resources we have in England. Changes in the world's climate are affecting the seasonal supply of water, making its management more and more critical. (p. 34)

- Freshwater ecosystems, which harbour the world's greatest concentration of species, are amongst the most vulnerable on Earth. (p. 35)

- Even in a country with a cool climate such as the UK, water is a limited resource. During hotter periods, shortages can quickly develop if we do not use water sparingly, particularly in more vulnerable parts of the country, such as the South East. So, are you using your water wisely? (p. 38)

- By following our top tips for saving water in the home and garden, you will soon be on the way to being 'waterwise'. (p. 38)

ADDITIONAL RESOURCES

You might like to contact the following organisations for further information. Due to the increasing cost of postage, many organisations cannot respond to enquiries unless they receive a stamped, addressed envelope.

CREATE
Kenley House
25 Bridgeman Terrace
Wigan, WN1 1TD
Tel: 01942 322271
Fax: 01942 322273
E-mail: info@create.org.uk
Web site: www.create.org.uk

ENCAMS (Environmental Campaigns)
Elizabeth House
The Pier
Wigan, WN3 4EX
Tel: 01942 824620
Fax: 01942 824778
E-mail: information@encams.org
Web site: www.encams.org and www.eco-schools.org.uk

English Nature
Northminster House
Northminster
Peterborough, PE1 1UA
Tel: 01733 455000 455101 enquiries
Fax: 01733 455103
E-mail: enquiries@english-nature.org.uk
Web site: www.english-nature.org.uk

The Environment Agency (HQ)
Rio House
Waterside Drive
Aztec West
Almondsbury
Bristol, BS12 4UD
Tel: 01454 624 400
Fax: 01454 624 409
Web site: www.environment-agency.gov.uk

Environmental Health News
Chadwick House Publishing
Chadwick Court
15 Hatfields
London, SE1 8DJ
Tel: 020 7928 6006
Fax: 020 7827 5866
E-mail: ehn@ehn-online.com
Web site: www.ehn-online.com

Friends of the Earth (FOE)
26-28 Underwood Street
London, N1 7JQ
Tel: 020 7490 1555
Fax: 020 7490 0881
E-mail: info@foe.co.uk
Web site: www.foe.co.uk and www.foei.org

Global Action Plan (GAP)
8 Fulwood Place, Gray's Inn
London, WC1V 6HG
Tel: 020 7405 5633
Fax: 020 7831 6244
E-mail: all@gappuk.demon.co.uk
Web site: www.globalactionplan.org.uk

International Food Policy Research Institute (IFPRI)
2033 K Street
N.W. Washington D.C. 20006
USA
Tel: + 1 202 862 5600
Fax: + 1 202 467 4439
E-mail: ifpri@cgiar.org
Web site: www.ifpri.org

The New Internationalist
55 Rectory Road
Oxford, OX4 1BW
Tel: 01865 728181
Fax: 01865 793152
E-mail: ni@newint.org
Web site: www.newint.org

People & the Planet
Planet 21
Suite 112, Spitfire Studios
63-71 Collier Street
London, N1 9BE
Tel: 020 7713 8108
Fax: 020 7713 8109
E-mail: planet21@totalise.co.uk
Web site: www.peopleandplanet.net

Tearfund
100 Church Road
Teddington
Middlesex, TW11 8QE
Tel: 020 8977 9144
Fax: 020 8943 3594
E-mail: enquiries@tearfund.org
Web site: www.tearfund.org

United Kingdom Committee for UNICEF
Africa House
64-78 Kingsway
London, WC2B 6NB
Tel: 020 7405 5592
Fax: 020 7405 2332
E-mail: info@unicef.org.uk
Web site: www.unicef.org.uk

WaterAid
Prince Consort House
27-29 Albert Embankment
London, SE1 7UB
Tel: 020 7793 4500
Fax: 020 7793 4545
E-mail: wateraid@wateraid.org
Web site: www.wateraid.org

WEA South Wales
7 Coopers Yard
Curran Road
Cardiff, CF10 5DF
Tel: 029 20235277
Fax: 029 20233986
E-mail: weasw@swales.wea.org.uk
Web site: www.swales.wea.org.uk

The Wildfowl and Wetlands Trust
Queen Elizabeth Walk, Barns
London, SW13 9WT
Tel: 020 8409 4400
Web site: www.wwtlearn.org.uk

WWF-International
Avenue Mont Blanc
CH-1196 Gland
Switzerland
Tel: + 41 22 364 91 11
Fax: + 41 22 364 88 36
Web site: www.panda.org

WWF-UK
Panda House
Weyside Park
Catteshall Lane
Godalming
Surrey, GU7 1XR
Tel: 01483 426444
Fax: 01483 426409
Web site: www.wwf.org.uk

INDEX

acid rain 11
agriculture
    and global water shortages 3, 4, 8
    and water management 18
    and water pollution 11
    water use by 36
aquifers, and global water supplies 7, 16, 19

biodiversity, loss of freshwater 35
businesses, investment in water-related projects 28

Camdessus report on the world water crisis 28
children
    in developing countries
        deaths and diseases from water-related illness 2, 3,
            5, 9, 13, 14
        and global water supplies 13-14
        and hygiene education 14
        and sanitation provision 13-14
        and water collection 13, 19-20
cholera 2, 12, 13, 32
climate change
    and global water supplies 1, 3, 5, 8
    and water management 34
CREATE, survey on water conservation 39

deaths, from water-related diseases 2, 9, 13, 14, 20, 35
deforestation, and water shortages 21, 36
desertification, and water shortages 21, 36
developing countries
    children and water collection 13-14
    and the right to water 24-5, 32
    and water collection 13, 19-20
    water pollution in 4, 10
    water and sanitation services 7, 8, 12, 17, 21
        and children 13-14
        costs of upgrading 20
        and development aid 30-1
        financing 31-2
    water shortages in 16, 19, 21
        and agriculture 3, 4
        and aid programmes 5
        statistics 2, 6, 7
diarrhoea
    and access to safe water and sanitation 17
    deaths from 14, 30
    and hygiene promotion 6, 12
    links to contaminated water 5, 12
disease
    water-related 2, 3, 5, 6, 9, 12, 19, 20, 35
        and children 2, 3, 5, 9, 13
        effects of 30-1

eco-systems
    degradation of freshwater 35
    and IRBM (integrated river basin management) 36

and water consumption 2, 16-17, 19
environmental improvements, and water bills 33, 34

food production, and global water supplies 3, 4, 7, 18

gardens, and water conservation 1, 36, 37, 38
GATS (General Agreements on Trade in Services), and
global water supplies 5, 23, 29
global water supplies 15-17
    financing the provision of 31-2
    and food production 3, 4, 7, 18
    and multinational water corporations 29-30
    and planned water management policies 8-9, 17
    projected worldwide water use 35
    statistics 1, 2, 4, 6, 8, 19, 20
    and water as a human right 24-5, 32
    and water pollution 10-11, 15
    and water shortages 15-17, 19, 21-2
        computer predictions of 3
        freshwater crisis 35-6
    water usage by sector 3
    and water users 36
    see also developing countries; water consumption;
water management

human rights, water as a human right 24-5, 32
hygiene education, in developing countries 6, 12, 13, 14

IFPRI (International Food Policy Research Institute),
and the impending water crisis 26-7
industry
    and water consumption 2, 8
    and water pollution 11
    water use by 36
IRBM (integrated river basin management) 36
irrigation
    and global water supplies 3, 4, 5, 19
    and inefficient water use 36
    and water conservation 27
    and water shortages 21
IWMI (International Water Management Institute), and
the impending water crisis 26-7

lakes
    drying up of 2
    pollution 4
        and freshwater supplies 15
living standards, and water consumption 8

malaria 6
manufacturing industry, use of water in 2, 8
multinational water corporations, and the privatisation
of water supplies 22, 23, 29-30

National Curriculum, and water 39
NGOs (non-governmental organisations), and global

ACKNOWLEDGEMENTS

The publisher is grateful for permission to reproduce the following material.

While every care has been taken to trace and acknowledge copyright, the publisher tenders its apology for any accidental infringement or where copyright has proved untraceable. The publisher would be pleased to come to a suitable arrangement in any such case with the rightful owner.

Chapter One: Global Concerns
Water – the big picture, © ENCAMS, *Facts about the global water shortage*, © 2003 Life Outreach International, *Computer predicts world water shortage*, © Environmental Health News 2003, *Worldwide water use*, © Reprinted with permission from the International Food Policy Research Institute and the International Water Management Institute, *Sustainable world – water*, © Sustainable World, *Water*, © Tearfund, *Water – the facts*, © 2003 New Internationalist, *Water statistics*, © 2003 New Internationalist, *Global water crisis*, © WEA South Sales, *Water quality*, © The Environment Agency 2003, *Water pollution*, © Geography Site, *Water*, © UNICEF, *Children and WaterAid*, © WaterAid, *Factfile statistics*, © WaterAid, *Fresh water: lifeblood of the planet*, © People & the Planet 200-2003, *Fresh water stress*, © World Meteorological Organisation (WMO), UNEP, *The food and water crisis*, © WWF-International, *A matter of life and death*, © United Nations, *Water availability versus population*, © UNESCO/IHP, *Water facts and figures*, © OECD, DFID, World Health Organisation, UNICEF.

Chapter Two: Global Solutions
Wet world drying, © The Wildfowl & Wetlands Trust, *The tide is high*, © Guardian Newspapers Limited 2003, *Water as a human right*, © WaterAid, *The impending water crisis and solutions to avert it*, © Reprinted with permission from the International Food Policy Research Institute and the International Water Management Institute, *Household water consumption*, © Reprinted with permission from the International Food Policy Research Institute and the International Water Management Institute, *Saving water*, © 2003 – UNESCO, *Prevention of the world water crisis*, © Guardian Newspapers Limited 2003, *Thirst for profits*, © Friends of the Earth International, *Priming the public pump*, © Guardian Newspapers Limited 2003, *Supplying water – for a price*, © United Nations, *Water bills to rise 70%*, © The Daily Mail, October 2003, *What they may charge*, © The Daily Mail, *Water bill could benefit wildlife sites*, © English Nature, *A global water crisis*, © WWF International, *Projected worldwide water use*, © Reprinted with permission from the International Food Policy Research Institute and the International Water Management Institute, *Frequently asked questions about water*, © Global Action Plan (GAP), *Sustainable water*, © Sustainable World, *Typical water use at home*, © Water UK 2003, *Waterwise in the home and garden*, © The Environment Agency 2003, *Water conservation in schools*, © The Environment Agency 2003, *Every drop counts*, © 2003 CREATE.

Photographs and illustrations:
Pages 1, 13, 21, 28: Simon Kneebone; pages 8, 18, 23: Pumpkin House; pages 10, 15, 25, 32: Bev Aisbett.

Craig Donnellan
Cambridge
January, 2004